CONFRONTING SEXUAL HARASSMENT

CONFRONTING SEXUAL HARASSMENT IN GHANAIAN UNIVERSITIES

AKUA OPOKUA BRITWUM
AND
NANA AMMA ANOKYE
Centre for Development Studies, University of Cape Coast,
Cape Coast, Ghana

GHANA UNIVERSITIES PRESS
ACCRA
2006

Published for

CENTRE FOR DEVELOPMENT STUDIES
UNIVERSITY OF CAPE COAST
CAPE COAST

by

Ghana Universities Press
P. O. Box GP 4219
Accra
Tel. 233(021) 513401
Fax 233(021) 513402

Distributed in Europe and North America
by African Books Collective Ltd
Unit 13 Kings Meadow
Ferry Hinksey Road
Oxford OX2 ODP
United Kingdom
E-mail: abc@africanbookscollective.com
Website: www.africanbookscollective.com

ISBN 13: 978-9964-30339-6

CONTENT

		Page
List of Tables		viii
List of Figures		viii
Preface		ix
List of Abbreviations		xi

1	**INTRODUCTION**	1
1.1	Background	1
1.2	The Study Problem	5
1.3	Rationale of the Study	6
1.4	Objectives of the Study	7
1.5	The Research Process	7
1.6	Structure of the Report	10

2	**EXPLAINING SEXUAL HARASSMENT**	12
2.1	Introduction	12
2.2	Definition	12
2.3	Categorising Sexual Harassment	14
2.4	Analyzing Sexual Harassment	17
2.5	Gender Power and Sexual Harassment	18
2.6	Culture and Sexual Harassment	21
2.7	Victim Blaming	22
2.8	Causes of Sexual Harassment	24
2.9	Sexual Harassment in Ghana	26

3	**PERCEPTIONS AND ATTITUDES TO SEXUAL HARASSMENT**	30
3.1	Introduction	30
3.2	The Respondents	30
3.3	Naming Sexual Harassment	33
3.4	Behaviours Classified as Sexual Harassment	35
3.5	Setting Tolerance Levels for Sexual Harassment	42
3.6	Perceptions about Possible Triggers of Sexual Harassment	44

3.7   Contesting General Notions of Sexual Harassment
Triggers   50
3.8   General Assumptions about Women   51

4   THE EXPERIENCE OF SEXUAL HARASSMENT   56
4.1   Introduction   56
4.2   Types of Sexual Harassment Experiences on University
Campuses   57
4.3   Sources and Location of Sexual Harassment Experiences   62
4.4   Likely Causes of Sexual Harassment   63
4.5   Reaction to Sexual Harassment   66
4.6   Effects of Sexual Harassment   68
4.7   Conclusion   70

**5   THE SEXUAL HARASSMENT MANAGEMENT
SYSTEM**   72
5.1   Introduction   72
5.2   Knowledge about Sexual Harassment Regulatory System   72
5.3   Departments/Sections Ever Used to Handle Sexual
Harassment   73
5.4   Entry Points for Developing University Sexual
Harassment Policies   77
5.5   Suggestions for Developing a Sexual Harassment Policy   79
5.5.1   Key Concerns for Managing Sexual Harassment   80
5.5.2   Suggestions for Preventing Sexual Harassment   81
5.5.3   Suggested Supporting Structures   83
5.5.4   Proof of University Commitment   84
5.6   Conclusion   85

**6   DEVELOPING UNIVERSITY BASED SEXUAL
HARASSMENT POLICIES: CHALLENGES
AND PROSPECTS**   86
6.1   Introduction   86
6.2   Highlights   86
6.3   Developing a University Based Sexual Harassment
Policy   89
6.3.1   Initiating the Process   89
6.3.2   The Content of a Sexual Harassment Policy   90
6.3.3   Implementing the Policy   92
6.4   Conclusion   98

concern for the administrative completion of the work went beyond a sense of duty. We single out for mention the following research assistants who undertook data gathering and the inputting of the data into computer for analysis: Maurice Kukuri, Fred, Alberta Konadu Owusu, Esther Afreh, Ahmed Baba, Emmanuel Abeka, Musa Dankwa and Ferdinand Adazuri (of blessed memory). Mr. Mohamed Tanko is also gratefully acknowledged for driving the personnel around the five public universisties for consultation, data gathering and the dissemination workshop.

We also recognize the assistance of Mr. Kwesi Boateng of KNUST and Mr. George Debrie of UDS and Mrs. Hamida of UG who acted as contact persons for the three main phases of the project. Mrs. Charlotte Braindt was responsible for co-ordinating all the numerous administrative and secretarial activities involved in organizing workshops in the five universisites. We are grateful to her.

Finally, we express our gratitude to the respondents and workshop participants, who gave up their time and effort to provide the needed input for this report.

AKUA O. BRITWUM
NANA AMMA ANOKYE

PREFACE

Ghanaian university campuses serve as educational communities and workplaces for several people of diverse backgrounds. The small number of females at all levels on university campuses makes sexual harassment policy an important tool for increasing female participation and promoting gender equality. Privatization of key university services like accommodation, meals and transportation opens the university campuses to large numbers of people outside the control of the university administration. This situation creates its own dynamics, and has to be managed with utmost care. The process of developing a policy can be fraught with several struggles if the issues are not clearly defined. The effectiveness of the final policy to achieve its intended goal is dependent on the manner in which the central issues are conceptualized. This publication highlights the current thinking on public university campuses in Ghana that directly affect the manner in which sexual harassment is perceived. Given that private universities are recent developments in Ghana, public universities still set the pace for determining the operations of universities. This publication, therefore, should provide all universities the framework to develop policies or review the ideas and principle underlying existing ones. It discusses the current attitudes and perceptions in relation to sexual harassment. Later chapters examine university structures for managing sexual harassment and offer some suggestions for developing university based policies. It is our hope that the issues raised will provide valuable information for the development of sexual harassment policies that will make the university campuses gender sensitive.

This report is the result of several efforts which we acknowledge. We acknowledge with gratitude the generous funding from the Ford Foundation, West African Office, which made the project possible. The vice-chancellors of the five public univerisites were very supportive in many memorable ways. We are grateful to them. The Director of the Centre for Development Studies, Prof. S. B.Kendie, provided ready collegial and administrative support throughout the entire project. His

LIST OF TABLES AND FIGURES

Table
3.1   Defining sexual harassment   34
3.2   Behaviours classified as sexual harassment   36
3.3   Respondents who think that sexual harassment is a
          serious violation of the rights of certain victims   40
3.4   Respondents perceptions about how to interpret
          females' negative response to male advances   49
3.5a   Common notions about women and work   53
3.5b   Common notions about females   54
4.1   Proportion of respondents who have experienced
          sexual harassment   58
4.2   Types of sexual harassment experienced on the
          campuses   59
4.3   Sex of harassers by causes of harassment   65
4.4   Behaviour of respondents interpreted as invitation
          to Harass   67
4.5   Effect of sexual harassment on victim   69
5.1   Departments/Sections ever used to manage sexual
          harassment cases   75
5.2   Respondents expressing satisfaction with facility
          ever used   77

Figures
3.1   Age of Respondents   31
3.2   Marital Status of Respondents   31
3.3a   Membership in groupings that meet regularly
          on-campus   32
3.3b   Membership in grouping that meet regularly off-campus   32
3.4a   Proportion of respondents finding harassing
          conditions unacceptable   43
3.4b   Proportion of respondents finding harassing
          conditions acceptable   43

LIST OF ABBREVIATIONS

AWLA	African Women's Lawyers Association
CHRAJ	Commission on Human Rights and Administrative Justice
FUSAG	Federation of University Staff Association of Ghana
GAUA	Ghana Association of University Administrators
GPRTU	Ghana Private Road Transport Union
GRASAC	Graduate Students' Association
KNUST	Kwame Nkrumah University of Science and Technology
NUGS	National Union of Ghana Students
SRC	Students' Representative Council
STDs	Sexually Transmitted Diseases
TEWU	Teachers and Educational Workers Union
UCC	University of Cape Coast
UCEW	University College of Education, Winneba
UDS	University for Development Studies
UE	University of Education
UG	University of Ghana
UTAG	University Teachers' Association of Ghana
WAJU	Women and Juvenile Unit

Notes   99

Appendices   101
Appendix 1   Targeted, Achieved Sample Size and Response
                     Rate   101
Appendix 2   Total Study Population   102
Appendix 3   Total Number of Workshop Participants   103
Appendix 4   Data Gathering Instruments   104
                     Questionnaire for Students   104
                     Questionnaire for University staff   116
                     Key Persons Interview Guide   131
                     Group Interview schedule   134
Appendix 5   Workshop Group Discussion Guides   135

References   139

Chapter 1

INTRODUCTION

Background

Sexual harassment, a problematic area in female and male relations, continues to attract attention within the general concern for gender equality (Brant and Too, 1994). The focus of attention derives from the gendered nature of sexually-harassing experiences. In addition, the experience of sexual harassment has been noted to create a hostile and demeaning work or study environment for the harassed (Brant and Too, 1994).

Delimiting the precise behaviours that make up sexual harassment remains a contested terrain (Brant and Too, 1994; University of Cape Town, 1994). Despite the disagreements it is generally accepted that sexual harassment covers behaviours at several levels that are unwanted and sexist in nature and have the effect of creating an intimidating, uncomfortable environment or a physically injurious impact (Brant and Too 1994; Wamahiu and Chege, 1996). The exact actions that make up behaviours considered sexually harassing range from verbal, non-verbal actions to direct physical assaults.

Sexual harassment is generally seen as a problem most likely to occur in the workplace or an educational institution. An exclusive focus on the experience of sexual harassment in the workplace and within educational institutions creates the impression that the phenomenon does not occur elsewhere. Brant and Too (1994) sound a warning about the tendency to refuse to recognize that sexual harassment can and does occur in other places such as the home and in the public space. However, the prevalence of sexual harassment in the occupational and educational settings merits attention in countries such as Ghana where attempts are being made to understand the problem.

Sexual harassment is not limited to one category of persons women, however, tend to suffer more than men (Wamahiu and Chege, 1996). Research results from several campuses and workplaces identify some conditions most likely to promote the occurrence of sexual harassment (*see* for example University of Cape Town, 1991). These studies revealed that an absence of a regulatory framework that sanctions harassers, community attitude that signifies tolerance, power and powerlessness, sexual ambivalence, as well as male dominance are important factors that promote sexual harassment.

Sexual harassment affects morale, job security, prospects for promotion, and health of workers. Students suffer effects similar to that which workers face; their morale is lowered and academic performance and social life are severely hampered. There can also be a general lack of confidence in the structures of authority governing an institution. The feelings of embarrassment, powerlessness, and the loss of self-confidence that such experiences might generate can lead to some level of cynicism about institutionalized authority. Though the direct victim of sexual harassment may be an individual, the range of its effects is much wider. The general response to the threat of sexual harassment is for the potential victims, mainly females, to make themselves unavailable through strategies they consider less likely to expose them to sexual harassment. The strategies they adopt restrict their ability to pursue and utilize university facilities at the same level and intensity as their male counterparts. Where the worker happens to be a major income earner for the home, family members also suffer. The behaviour of non-victims becomes circumscribed by what others have suffered and people find themselves performing or shunning specific acts in order to avoid getting harassed.

Sexual harassment in educational institutions is of particular concern because of the threat it presents to the development of human resource capacities. Education provides the opportunity for personal advancement especially in terms of the career openings it offers. University education is crucial in this sense because of the level of human resource capacity that it develops and utilizes. It is important that members of university communities are provided with the chance to function in an environment devoid of experiences that inhibit their ability to operate at their fullest potential. In Ghana where universities tend to be residential, their activities are extensive, providing not only numero... chances for educational advancement for the students it admits, but career openings for its numerous employees. Universities in Ghana present both the workplace and the educational contexts within which sexual harassment can occur.

Ghanaian universities remain male preserves despite efforts at national and institutional levels to increase female participation. In 1996, for example, the proportion of female academics in the three main universities (University of Cape Coast, and University of Ghana, as well as the Kwame Nkrumah University of Science and Technology) was 12.1 per cent. The male proportion in the early 1990s was as high as 91.2 per cent (Brown *et al.*, 1996). At the time of the study the highest proportion of female students (34 per cent) was recorded at the University of Ghana (UG) whilst the lowest (16 per cent) was recorded at the University for Development Studies (UDS) (*see* Appendix 1). Female teaching staff proportion followed a similar trend, the highest proportion of 20 per cent was recorded again at UG and the lowest (6.9 per cent) at UDS. Kwame Nkrumah University of Science and Technology (KNUST) had a proportion of 7 per cent. In all, the proportion of females in the universities was around 19 per cent. Not only is female proportion of the university population low, it was declining at the University of Cape Coast. At the University of Cape Coast (UCC) the proportion of female teaching staff fell to 10.6 per cent in 2001 and later to 10.3 per cent in 2002 after reaching 12.7 per cent in 1997. For students the highest ever reached was 26.8 per cent in 1998, it stood at 26.7 per cent in 2002. Non-teaching staff proportion also showed a similar declining trend from a high of 22.5 per cent in 1997 to 18.9 per cent in 2002.

Most studies on sexual harassment in Ghana have been mainly students' dissertations that have a campus specific focus. In terms of space and focus, most studies have been confined to one campus and examined the relationship of specific factors to sexual harassment. Others have focused generally on abuse and violence against females at the basic and secondary schools. Fiscian *et al.* (2003), for example, studied the incidence and prevalence of sexual harassment in Ghanaian Basic Schools. The ground-breaking publication from the Gender Studies and Human Rights Documentation Centre (Coker-Appiah and Cusack, 1999) contains sections on sexual harassment as one of the numerous forms of violence against women and children. The recent study undertaken by the African Women's Lawyers Association (AWLA) presents a major attempt to study sexual harassment in the Ghanaian workplace (AWLA, 2003).

Ghanaian newspapers give coverage to the incidence of sexual harassment through case and opinion reports. A publication in *The Mirror* in 1998, for example, presented the views of seven people of different backgrounds on sexual harassment. The interview in the newspaper revealed a growing concern for a need to confront sexual harassment in all its manifestations in Ghana. In 1999, the *Public Agenda* covered extensively judgement on a case by the Ghanaian Human Rights Administrator, which awarded damages to a female victim of workplace sexual harassment. Such publications serve to highlight the existence of sexual harassment and the paucity of knowledge about the nature of sexual harassment in the country.

As preparation towards a comprehensive research on the nature and experience of sexual harassment in Ghanaian universities, the Centre for Development Studies (CDS), a research institution at University of Cape Coast, organized a one-day workshop in December 1998. Participants for the workshop were drawn from the main sectors of the (Micah, *et al* 1998) university, namely, students, lecturers and administrators as well as personnel in charge of general university policy and the management of student affairs. The workshop focused on the problem on the UCC campus with the view that a preliminary appraisal of sexual harassment on the UCC campus would form a useful basis for designing a more comprehensive study of the problem in all universities in Ghana. Such a study would investigate the nature and extent of sexual harassment in universities as the basis for evolving a framework that will provide the setting for policy formulation.

The workshop identified sexual harassment at UCC as verbal or physical behaviours that are threatening, offensive, unwelcome, and based on negative gender perceptions. Participants at the workshop concluded that the incidence of sexual harassment was pervasive on the UCC campus in both the workplace and educational settings. All members of the community were subject to different levels of sexual harassment. Female students, however, suffered more in terms of frequency and intensity.

The workshop also identified the following as attitudes, norms and traditions at UCC that encourage sexual harassment:

1. Perceptions about what acceptable modes of behaviour by women should be.
2. The absence of an administrative framework for dealing with sexual harassment and act as a deterrent to prospective harassers.
3. Inadequate accommodation for students and overcrowding in the halls of residence.

4. Students' celebrations that centre on obscenities and the display of pornography as well as those that call for modes of dressing considered inappropriate in females.
5. Lack of support from friends and colleagues and fear that if exposed a "powerful" harasser might resort to intimidating the victim.
6. Recourse to amicable settlement outside formal structures of the university for handling disciplinary issues.
7. Guilt on the part of the victim for the pain perpetrators will suffer on having to face punishment reserved for sexual harassers.

The workshop noted with concern that the management of sexual harassment was not separate from the main administrative structures for handling all other disciplinary issues. The result is that the process becomes long-winded and the deterrent effect of sanctions greatly reduced. The structures for handling disciplinary issues also lean heavily towards personal inputs rather than on the dynamics of the principles that underlie them. The conclusion was that sexual harassment on the university campuses should be subjected to a comprehensive study in order to unravel its dynamics.

The Study Problem

The study by Coker-Appiah and Cusack (1999) on violence against women and children in Ghana revealed that most victims of sexual harassment were reporting their experiences to friends, parents, and other relatives. There was hardly any recourse to report experiences to more formalized structures where sanctions would be more severe and also serve to highlight the occurrence of the problem. In addition, there appears to be some difficulty in assessing the nature and extent of sexual harassment, as the perceptions of people on the subject tends to be clouded by several other related issues.

The UCC workshop in 1998 pointed out the need for a university-based policy for effectively managing sexual harassment. The absence of the required policy seems to suggest an abdication of the responsibility of the university to protect its members and a tacit endorsement of the violation of their rights (Heise, Heise *et al.* 1995). The need for a policy has not been disputed; what is lacking is an understanding of the issues at stake and how the development of a policy should proceed. A policy on sexual harassment will have to cover procedures for sensitizing the community and the problems of discipline that emanate from the incidence of sexual harassment on the university campus. The background for developing such a policy has to be informed by research that enhances the understanding of the nature and extent of sexual harassment as well as the perceptions that members of the community have.

Rationale of the Study

University education is considered the apex of educational attainment. All who get exposed to this form of education expect not only to gain knowledge from the formal teaching, which occurs in the lecture halls, but also to benefit from the experiences that informal interaction among peers, superiors and juniors can bring. The social environment within a university should, therefore, be one that stimulates and encourages the development of a critical attitude to life. The environment should generate the formation of strong personalities who are ready to confront the world and the challenges it brings. It becomes the responsibility of all concerned with university education to ensure that the social environment is devoid of events that might hinder the attainment of such goals.

The occurrence of sexual harassment in universities generates concern. This is because it has been established in several instances that sexual harassment inhibits the ability of members to participate fully in university activities (University of Cape Town, 1994). Sexual harassment affects an individual's self esteem and as a result has a negative impact on the victim's work or academic performance. Universities are in a unique position because they not only give employment to high-level personnel but train them as well. A good policy on sexual harassment will reduce its incidence and help to improve qualitatively the participation of females in higher education. A high level of awareness of the nature and impact of sexual harassment on university activities will lead to the production of large numbers of high-level personnel highly sensitized before they enter into the job market outside the university. This group of personnel sensitive to sexual harassment will be better predisposed to measures designed to tackle sexual harassment in the wider community. As employers, the universities stand in a good position to set the pace for the broader public in terms of the guidelines they outline to deal with sexual harassment and how the policy gets reformed and strengthened to handle the challenges that all new procedures are bound to face.

Objectives of the Study

The main objective of the study was to investigate the nature and extent of sexual harassment as the basis for assisting in the development of university-based policies on sexual harassment. Specific objectives of the study were:

1. Identifying forms of sexual harassment that occur on the university campuses;
2. Describing the experiences of sexual harassment on the university campuses;
3. Examining attitudes and perceptions of members of the university community towards sexual harassment;
4. Assessing the institutional capacity of the universities for handling cases of sexual harassment;
5. Identifying provisions within the universities that can form the basis for developing policies to manage sexual harassment.

The Research Process

The study began with a series of consultations with key persons like administrative personnel, interest groups representatives like University Teachers' Association of Ghana (UTAG)[1], the Students' Representative Council (SRC)[2], the National Union of Ghanaian Students (NUGS)[3], Federation of University Senior Staff Association of Ghana (FUSSAG)[4], Ghana Association of University Administrators (GAUA)[5] and Teachers and Educational Workers Union (TEWU), Deans of Students, personnel of the Counselling Centres and some deans of faculties in all five public universities in Ghana. The consultation was aimed at getting information from key sectors of the communities as to their conception of the relevance of the research and what issues they considered important for a research on sexual harassment to cover. The need for this study on the other campuses was affirmed. The view generally was that the study should cover the following:

1. The definition and forms of sexual harassment;
2. Levels, trends, and the intensity of occurrence;
3. Assumptions and perceptions and employment issues;
. 4. The experience, causes, sources and the impact suffered;
5. · The most vulnerable members;
6. The university management of sexual harassment;
7. Sexuality and mode of dressing.

These themes informed the final outcome of the types of instruments and the issues that items on the instruments covered. Three main methods of data collection were used, namely, questionnaire administration, individual and key informant interviews as well as group interviews. The survey methods were used to collect information on specific incidence, and levels of prevalence of sexually-harassing practices within 'he various sections of the university community as well as the perceptions of sexual harassment on the campuses. The specific instruments employed in data collection were the individual, group and key informant interview schedules, and a record schedule for examining documents (*see* Appendix 2).

The population of the study consisted of the entire university community of all public universities in Ghana. These universities were the University of Cape Coast (UCC), University of Education, Winneba[7] (UEW), University for Development Studies (UDS), University of Ghana (UG), and Kwame Nkrumah University of Science and Technology (KNUST). Students, teaching and non teaching staff were studied as district groups.

As mentioned earlier, female representation in Ghanaian universities is generally, low. The selection of the study sample was carried out with care in order to ensure equal representation of both female and male respondents. Sampling was, therefore, based on the female population on the various campuses. UDS, the smallest university, had a population of 707 students at the time of the study. The others had student population sizes ranging from 6000 at UEW to over 14000 for UG in 2000. Ten per cent of the female student population was sampled together with an equivalent number of males. At UDS where the female student population was below 100, the entire number was selected with an equivalent number of males. Quota sampling was used to arrive at the total sample for each Faculty/Institute/School, and Halls of Residence. In 2000, female non-teaching staff proportion ranged from 18 per cent at KNUST to 22 per cent at UEW. For this group, the sample proportion selected was slightly higher, 20 per cent of the females with equivalent numbers of males was selected. Quota sampling was used to select respondents from the faculties/institutes/schools and the support units. The relative number of female teaching staff in all the universities was the lowest, so the whole population of females was selected with equivalent number of males in the various ranks and faculties/institutes/school.

Key informants constituted another category of respondents that were covered. Selection was not based on sex but rather on the position of the informants. They were drawn from university policy makers, student affairs managers, counselling centre personnel, members of university disciplinary committees and student leaders. In all, 2,175 respondents were covered in the study. Of this number, 1,119 were females and 1056 were males. Out of the 2,175, 1,425 were students, 462 non-teaching staff and 217 teaching staff. The number of key persons covered was 71. On the whole, it was possible to achieve a sex balance in terms of respondents' background although the spread was not even on the various campuses (Appendix 1).

The timing of the study greatly affected the availability of respondents especially on the UG campus where students were just about to take their examinations. On the other campuses, the duration of the study posed a challenge especially for the teaching staff where most preferred to fill in the instruments themselves rather than being interviewed. In some instances, they were unable to complete the instrument for collection before the departure of the research team. Some respondents kept their word and posted the instrument to the research team at their base at the Centre for Development Studies. On campuses where it had been impossible to reach the targeted female/male sample balance attempts were made to reach that balance on the next campus. In most instances, more instruments were distributed than required and this resulted in offsetting the targeted balance.

The primary and secondary data were put into themes such as the definition of sexual harassment, forms and the experience of sexual harassment. Other themes that were distilled for purposes of data analysis were individual and institutional attitudes to sexual harassment as well as institutional management of sexual harassment. The organization of data in this way was used to establish trends and possible occurrence of events. Statistical measures of central tendency, proportions and sheer frequencies were used to organize data for interpretation. Peculiar cases were interpreted on their own merits.

The final stage was a series of dissemination workshops held at UCC (April 7, 2003), UG (April 10, 2003), KNUST (April 22, 2003), UDS (April 24, 2003) and at UEW (May 26, 2003). The aim of the workshops were first, to present and discuss with the university communities the research findings and second to deliberate on the concerns that a framework for managing sexual harassment in each university should address. Participants at these workshops were made up of interest group representatives, and frontline personnel in university decision-making structures (*see* Appendix 5 for Total Number of participants). There was a total of 292 participants at the workshops, 121 were females and 171 males. Student participants were 101, teaching staff participants 83 and non-teaching staff participants 108 (*see* Appendix 1).

Structure of the Report

The report has been organized into six main chapters. The first chapter which is the introduction begins with a background and presents the problem investigated and objectives that guided the study as well as the research process. The second chapter examines the core issues making up sexual harassment as well as the experience of others elsewhere.

The main body of the report which consist of an analysis of findings from the field are presented in the third, fourth and fifth chapters. The third chapter is a description of the background of respondents in terms of their age, and marital status and a discussion of respondents' definition of sexual harassment and the specific understanding of behaviours they identify as sexually-harassing. Attitude to sexual harassment and the assumptions that feed these attitudes on the campuses are examined in this chapter as well. The fouth chapter present the manner in which sexsual harassment is experienced on the university compus. The various forms that members of the university community have been confronted with, their response as well as what they perceive to be the underlying factors and their response. The impact a sexually-harassing event has on members of the university community is also discussed in this chapter.

The fifth describes the policy environment and the institutional capacity of the various universities for managing sexual harassment. The chapter captures both the field data and the outcome of the dissemination workshops on the university campuses. The final chapter highlights the main findings and identifies the conditions within which an efficient University Sexual Harassment Management Policy can be developed.

Chapter 2

EXPLAINING SEXUAL HARASSMENT

Introduction

Henry and Meltzoff (1998) describe sexual harassment as a form of victimization of or discrimination against women that has occurred throughout history. Before the 1970s, however, events currently identified as sexual harassment were considered personal and, therefore, attracted individual solutions. It was Lin Farley's consciousness-raising session with working women in the US that first put the term sexual harassment on an established footing (Brandt and Too, 1994). According to Brant and Too's account the participants agreed that the common experience of unpleasant and unwanted behaviour from men that they all shared in their places of work required a name. Sexual harassment was the term that came closest to characterizing the phenomenon. Since 1976, sexual harassment has been highlighted by feminists, trade unionists and later human right activists, who have succeeded in making it a social problem. The range of behaviours it covers have broadened and so have the contexts within which its occurrence raises concerns. Giving a name to sexual harassment translated into challenging it as an accepted behaviour. These and subsequent developments helped to legitimize sexual harassment as a social problem affecting equal opportunity for educational and employment development of females

Definition

Like all social issues, sexual harassment has several defi itions. The definitions are as varied as the sources from which they arise. Aeberhard-Hodges (1997) points out that most of the definitions of sexual harassment combine three main elements. The first is the perception of the person at the receiving end and the interpretation of the behaviour as unwanted and/or sexual in nature. Here attempts are made to distinguish sexual harassment from behaviour that is welcome and mutual. The second element is the intention of the harasser; in this case, an action is sexually harassing if, in addition to the above, it becomes a condition for receiving some benefit or has the tendency to humiliate. The third is the impact that a sexually-harassing act creates; an offensive or hostile environment or physical injury for the harassed. Some definitions tend to provide the location of the event as the workplace or an educational institution.

The terms: unwanted, unwelcome or unsolicited feature in almost all definitions of sexual harassment. Definitions such as that supplied by ILO (1992), Aeberhard-Hodges (1997), Brant and Too (1994), Wamahiu and Chege (1996) and the Labour Act 2003 (Act 651) all stress the unwelcome nature of the sexual advances/behaviour. The perception of a person at the receiving end of a sexually-harassing event is critical in deciding what does or does not constitute sexual harassment. For Dall'Ara and Maass (1999), most legal analyses suggest that the subjective interpretations of the harassed play an essential role in determining whether an experience is sexually harassing or not.

An act can be considered sexually-harassing when it violates certain conditions. Some forms of social conduct, however, are not inherently offensive and the reactions they solicit can be ambiguous (Reinhart, 1999). The acceptability of the conduct is dependent on the manner in which it is perceived by the recipient. Reinhart acknowledges that sexual attraction plays a significant role in daily social exchanges between employees. The distinction between an invited and unwanted conduct sometimes falls into a "grey area". The distinguishing feature in this instance is the psychological reaction of the receiving party for whom the conduct creates a hostile environment because it is demeaning, unreciprocated, one sided or imposed. In recognition of the difficulty in determining when acceptable daily social encounters become sexual harassment, some top companies covered in an ILO survey in 1999 prohibit "romantic conduct/liaisons" between their employees (Reinhart, 1999). For Bortei-Doku Aryeetey (2004), however, the distinction between non-coercive (based on mutual desire and attraction), and coercive (driven by harassment founded on power) sexuality in the workplace is instructive because it draws attention to the abuse of sex to gain advantage in the workplace.

Definitions such as those provided by the ILO (1994) and AWLA Ghana (2003) stress the subjective nature of the experience in addition to its negative impact. Other definitions whilst highlighting the subjective nature of the experience also recognize sexual features of the action and the sex of the one at the receiving end (Aeberhard-Hodges, 1997). The origin of the term and subsequent events, however, lead to a spatial restriction of some definitions. Thus, some definitions tend to add that the event must have occurred in a work or educational context or both (Stein, 1993).

The defining features are finally that the acts are sexual in nature, unwanted, intimidating or demeaning, and make the environment in which one operates hostile. The position of Reilly, *et al.* (1999) that obtaining an appropriate working definition of sexual harassment that takes into consideration many perceptions is a necessary first step in studying and reducing the problem is worth considering. A clear and concise definition is important for removing some of the likely problems that might arise from managing sexual harassment like ambiguities and adequate provision of protection for those most vulnerable.

Categorizing Sexual Harassment

Once sexsual harassment has been defined the next problem that arises is isolating the specific behavours that should be labelled as sexsual-harassing. This arises from the fact that subjectivity comes to play in determining whether or not an action is sexually-harassing. There is also the role that cross cultural perspectives can play in determining which behaviours can pass for sexual harassment. Many women and men experience behaviours ordinarily identified as sexually-harassing as pleasurable. Having to label some experiences as sexually-harassing, they contend, forces people to draw a line between illicit and legitimate forms of sexuality within institutions. The process they admit is sometimes fraught with ambiguity since the main factors that determine whether or not a particular interaction will be identified as sexually-harassing are first the intention of the harasser and secondly the interpretation of the interchange by the harassed. Both of which, are influenced by workplace and institutional culture and the social context of the events (Guiffre and Williams, 1994). Guiffre and Williams (1994) observe that many victims fail to report cases of sexual harassment because they do not recognize sexual harassment as an actionable offence.

These difficulties notwithstanding, there is some broad agreement about the group of behaviours labelled as sexually-harassing. Sexually-harassing behaviours broadly take five main forms (Reinhart, 1999). Sexual harassment can be physical in nature; where people are touched, pinched, patted or even kissed without their consent or physically assaulted or raped. Secondly, sexual harassment can be verbal when people are subjected to verbal assaults or intimidation, unwelcome comments, jokes and insinuations or sexually-explicit conversations or suggestive comments. Gestural harassment takes the form of sexually suggestive gestures, whereas emotional harassment consists of behaviours which isolate, and are discriminatory towards, a person on the grounds of his or her sex. The last form identified, written or graphic harassment, involves sending pornographic pictures through e-mail, posting pin-ups or addressing unwanted love letters to a person.

The specific events that constitute harassment are, generally, categorized into two: those that create a hostile environment like unwanted sexual attention including gender harassment and sexual coercion which includes *quid pro quo* harassment (Dall'Ara and Maass, 1999; Henry and Meltzoff, 1998; Reinhart, 1999). Gender harassment, alternatively called misogyny by Dall'Ara and Maass (1999), includes verbal and nonverbal behaviours that convey insulting, hostile or degrading attitudes towards women without aiming at sexual co-operation. The common examples they cite are the diffusion of pornographic materials, sexual epithets, insults and gestures made with the intent to offend women. Gender harassment also includes seductive behaviour in the form of unwanted, inappropriate and offensive physical or verbal sexual advances.

Other forms of hostile environment sexual harassment include unwelcome sexual advances, requests for sexual favours and other verbal, nonverbal or physical conduct of a sexual nature by an employee, another student or a third party. They become harassing behaviours when they are sufficiently severe, persistent or pervasive so as to limit a student or worker's ability to participate in or benefit from an educational or occupational programme or activity or create a hostile or abusive environment (Dall'Ara and Maass, 1999).

Quid pro quo harassment is the threat of harm or promise of reward which is offered in return for sex (Henry and Meltzoff, 1998). For Heise *et al.* (1999), sexual coercion exists along a continuum from forcible rape to non-physical forms of pressure that compel girls and women to engage in sex against their will. *Quid pro quo* harassment, therefore, comes in the form of sexual coercion (threats) or sexual bribery or favouritism involving the solicitation of sexual activity or other sex-linked behaviour by promise of a reward (Fitzgerald and Shullman, 1993). It involves situations in a school or workplace when students' or workers' participation in an educational or occupational event is conditional to their submission to unwelcome sexual advances or requests for sexual favours. In this instance, it is inconsequential if a student or worker resists and suffers the threatened harm or submits and avoids the threatened harm; the condition is devoid of options. The touchstone of sexual coercion, Heise *et al.* (1999) explain, is that a woman lacks choices and faces severe physical or social consequences if she resists the sexual advances.

Good (1999) admits that the use of academic authority to acquire sexual favours or the offer of professional support for sex is an unwanted, intrusive relationship between unequals. It involves a betrayal of responsibility by academic staff to students and to the scholarly practice based on learning and trust. For her, the power exercised by the professor in giving praise or blame, grades and recommendations greatly diminishes the student's freedom of choice. A similar observation can be made in the work situation involving the boss and worker.

The flip side of sexual bribery is sexual corruption. Pereira (2002) describes this as the situation where females aggressively seek sexual relationships in exchange for gifts and money and other social resources. Bortei-Doku Aryeetey (2004) explains that in the power struggle associated with gender politics, women are not oblivious of the use of sex as a weapon or bait. Fear that they might not be able to compete on the basis of performance and competence drive some women to use *sponsored mobility* consciously adopting "seductive strategies in their negotiations with men" (p.11) as an alternative route to progress. Sponsored mobility can benefit men as well. Workers of both sexes have utilized means other than sexuality to gain advantage over their colleagues. Even though males claim that females harass them this way, men still have control, for they hold what the women need and the women have to negotiate for that resource. Females in this situation harass from a position of vulnerability with no escape from the loss of dignity, or low self-esteem that the need for the resource they pursue by peddling sexual favours bring. Prah in her presentation at the dissemination workshop on the UCC campus explained that sexual corruption is a manifestation of women's low status and a survival strategy[8].

Henry and Meltzoff (1998) note that *quid pro quo* harassment which encompasses those behaviours that are generally agreed upon as sexual harassment attracts very little disagreement. The hostile environment sexual harassment, however, is surrounded by controversy as a result of the subjective judgement of the harassed which is the determining factor (Henry and Meltzoff, 1998). What is deemed as unwelcome is subject to the individual's interpretation of the perpetrator's behaviour. They explain that what is offensive and considered to be sexual harassment to one individual may not be to another.

Categorizing sexual harassment in literature is less contentious than is the case in real life situations where people have to make a distinction and label some experiences as sexually-harassing. Reilly, *et al.* (1999) and Livingstone (1979) explain that several factors beyond the act itself affect people's perception in determining whether behaviour is sexual harassment or not. Factors like the age of the persons involved for example people's social status and gender all affect how they identify sexually-harassing interactions. Females, for example, tend to categorize more kinds of behaviours as sexual harassment and are more affected by certain behaviours when their harassers hold a higher status.

Analyzing Sexual Harassment

A variety of perspectives provide theoretical explanation of sexual harassment. There are those who place sexual harassment within the social deviant perspective and therefore see sexual harassment as aspects of deviant behaviour. Exhibition of sexually-harassing behaviour is the result of inability to conform. Social psychologists take the medical psychoanalytic approach and read into sexual harassment pathological state of the harassed or the harasser. The pathological state, caused by childhood experiences, stress, drugs, or even some inborn condition, like defective genes or hormones, have been offered as possible explanations to sexual harassment. Koss and Cleveland (1997) observe that such approaches tend to portray the erroneous view that sexual aggression, as a problem, is caused by a pathological few in society. But the pervasiveness of the problem attests to the contrary.

Sexual harassment, according to the Marxist perspective, is the result of capitalism. Women's subordination is an essential feature of capitalist exploitation of labour and sexual harassment a useful weapon for enforcing that subordination (Young, 1993). In social exchange theory, sexual harassment becomes an essential feature in the exchange of resources. It is the lack of resources that makes an individual susceptible to sexual harassment. For feminists, however, the best explanation for sexual harassment is patriarchy, male power over females (Bhasin, 1993). Within patriarchy, male power is not a property that is owned but rather a relation that structures interactions between women and men in all spheres of life. Sexual harassment features as essentially patriarchal and becomes one of the forms in which male power over females is expressed and maintained. The feminist perspective offers the best explanation for several questions that sexual harassment pose such as why victims are overwhelmingly female and perpetrators male or why sex becomes so prominent in male relations with women and finally why in some instances a just cause for sexual harassment has been found (Bhasin, 1993).

Feminists' acknowledgement of male power being at the centre of sexual harassment has been criticized as constituting victim feminism. Observers like Gallop, according to Good (1999), reject victim feminism because they believe that women have the capacity to choose how to express their sexuality. Women are free to express their sexuality, and are not mere sexual objects of men's sexual impulses. Thus, banning all amorous relations between students and professors, as has been the case of some universities in the US as a measure for dealing with sexual harassment, is dehumanizing because it reinforces women's status as objects rather than desiring subjects. Theories devoted to explaining sexual harassment point to ways in which sexual harassment can be addressed in order to enhance women's participation in the educational and professional environment.

Gender Power and Sexual Harassment

Like other forms of gender-based violence, sexual harassment is gendered in terms of its victims and perpetrators (Aeberhard-Hodges, 1997; Heise, *et al;* 1999; Brandt and Too, 1994). According to Kadalie and Flood (1996), anyone can be verbally or physically assaulted on the basis of his/her sex or sexual identity. However, despite the fact that the experience of sexual harassment is not limited to one category of persons, women on the whole tend to suffer more the incidence of sexual harassment than men and the perpetrators are overwhelmingly male (Wamahiu and Chege, 1996). This observation, according to Heise, Moore and Touba (1995), has only recently received attention. Aeberhard-Hodges (1997) recognizes that more and more cases of women being harassed by other women are coming up but an overwhelming number of victims are women who have been harassed in one form or other by men.

The explanation of the gendered nature of sexual harassment has been attributed to patriarchy, male power over females. The different forms sexual harassment takes, Kelly (1988) contends, are connected to the central objective of the perpetrator, which is to achieve power and control over the victim. Sexual harassment, viewed this way, is categorized as part of a continuum of behaviour that occurs within the context of unequal social relations, particularly between women and men. This continuum begins with sexual harassment, moves to battering and rape through to murder. Sexual harassment as a form of violence against women becomes a product of women's unequal status and in turn reinforces and helps to maintain that unequal status (McKinnon 1979).

Sexual harassment is, primarily, an issue of power and not sex as we have noted early. It occurs when a person with power abuses that power, breaching the trusting relationship that normally exists between students and others in an academic institution. Attempts made to confront the issue at the University of Cape Town indicate that most of the people who have been subjected to some form of sexual harassment have experienced it within the context of power relations. Such people have a feeling of powerlessness, which occurs in situations such as gender harassment amongst peers, students and their professors as well as workers and their bosses.

The conditions that combine to make women particularly vulnerable to sexual harassment is their gendered position that makes them subordinate in society as well as their economic and political status on one hand, and, on the other, male dominance in all spheres of life. Women's vulnerability to sexual harassment is aggravated by their lower social standing as regards age, employment and academic positions and their higher need to earn a living (Aeberhard-Hodges 1997; Desouza, *et al;* 1998; McKinnon, 1979). Such conditions render women powerless. Power is, therefore, reflected in women's lack of it as exemplified in their subordinate position and at the same time in male power exaggerated by their dominance in the work and academic situations. According to Tete-Mensah, Paludi and Defour categorize such power differentials as superior/subordinate power[9]. Women's attempt to ward off sexual harassment advances is constrained by their vulnerability and male power which is most of the time backed by institutional authority.

For Guiffre and Williams (1994), in any situation where power is vested in the male, the lower position of the female plus the sexual potential of her body act to make her an easy victim of sexual harassment. Opportunity structures within the hierarchical workplace provide people who occupy positions of authority the occasion to use their legitimate power to compel persons of lower positions to submit to their sexual demands. Sexual harassment of women is possible as a result of the power that men have over women and also as a form of control over women. Sexual harassment is the medium through which male power is expressed and the tool for maintaining power over women (McKinnon, 1979). Men have power over women and use that power to sexually-harass women. Harassing women sexually also becomes a tool for maintaining their power over women (Bhasin, 1993). Male power is usually strengthened by their ascribed positions in the workplace and academic situation as bosses, professors or their sheer numbers in male dominated work and educational institutions.

Dawene (1985) makes a distinction between the power element at play in sexual harassment in the workplace and the university setting. He acknowledges that power relations between students and lecturers are more pronounced because students are dependent on lecturers for their grades, recommendations and research opportunities. The age differential between students and their professors is wider and students who are relatively young look up to their professors with awe and are more likely to misinterpret sexual advances from their professors. Being older, workers are generally more likely to recognize sexual harassment advances. The educational setting within the university, however, provides more options for students to cope with sexual harassment than the workplace. Female students who are sexually-harassed can drop out of courses without suffering serious consequences. Workers might find it impossible to leave a job and as a result are forced to tolerate sexual harassment. Thus, the more pronounced power differentials, between students and their lecturers is mitigated by the presence of better coping strategies which the workplace does not offer. Institutional power and its role in giving opportunity to males in authority to harass should be a key area of concern in any policy on sexual harassment.

The explanation of male power at the centre of sexual harassment provides a useful tool in the understanding of why sexual harassment, like other forms of gender-based violence, is mainly perpetrated by men against women. Beyond making females easy victims of sexual harassment, male power and women's vulnerability constrain their response to sexual harassment. Studies devoted to understanding why women keep silent and refuse to report their abusive experience, have identified a sense of shame, a feeling of responsibility for the action and women's fear of reprisals (Dobash and Dobash, 1992) as the main factors. The power element at play within sexual harassment provides a useful distinction between female and male sexual harassers. Prah[10] pointed out in her presentation on the overview of sexual harassment in Ghana that structural inequality in gender relation gives males power which they use to harass females. Female harassers, on the other hand, harass males from a position of powerlessness.

Gendered power relations provide males useful ammunition to harass females even from positions of lower institutional status, contra power sexual harassment. Male students for, example, harass female lecturers from this position as means of undermining the institutional authority of the female lecturers. Male power in peer harassment is sometimes buttressed by their overwhelming numbers in workplace and academic institutions. When females are in the minority in such institutions they easily feel intimidated[11]. In peer harassment, males derive power to harass females of equal institutional status from gender power. Victims of contra-power and peer harassment stand a better chance of warding of sexually harassing advances.

Culture and Sexual Harassment

Almost all societies have indigenous moral codes that could be used against the sexual violation of women and no religion or social code of ethics condone or openly support sexsual voilence (Heise, *et al;* 1995). Most cultures, however, have beliefs, norms and social institutions that legitimize and therefore perpetuate violence against women. Justification for violence against women often evolves from social or gender norms about the proper roles and responsibilities of women and men (*ibid*).

Heise, *et al.,* affirm that a consistent list of events which sexual harassment studies world wide have identified as provoking violence constitute a transgression of gender norms. As a result it is always possible to find, in all cultures, the notion of a "just cause" that is used to absolve harassers from the responsibility of having committed an offence. Societies are often able to distinguish between just and unjust reasons for violence as well as between acceptable and unacceptable levels of aggression against women for having transgressed gender norms (Heise *et al.,* 1995). In our particular instance, it is the case of female mode of dressing which is seen as provoking a sexually-harassing reaction from males.

Of particular interest here are notions of decency in sexuality and the expressions of it which serve as a "just cause" for sexual harassment. A study at the University of Cape Town identified some ambivalence about sexual norms that young people carry. Males on the whole are expected to be promiscuous and the number of sexual escapades that males have had forms the basis of acceptance into certain circles. Females, on the other hand, are expected to be chaste, what Koss and Cleveland (1997) describe as sexual gatekeepers, and to steer clear of sexual activity outside of a committed relationship. All women as a result are expected to put up a show of refusing sexual advances and it becomes a man's job to overcome the feigned protest. Token resistance is the situation where men believe that women frequently say "no" to sexual advances when in fact they mean "yes".

One way in which male dominance is reflected in the experience of sexual harassment is the attempt to impose male perceptions of decency and sexuality on women by determining what is provocative and as such what is decent in dressing styles (Aeberhard-Hodges, 1997, Twumasi, 2002). Cultural norms and values, therefore, inform sexual harassment. Social interactions that form the mechanisms for transmitting social values and norms at the base of sexual harassment is learned, as a result the social rules that govern sexual relations differ from society to society and according to cultures. Ideas of behaviours that surround sexual behaviour change over time and in conformity with the dynamism of cultures. For Heise *et al.,* (1995), although culture can and does aggravate women's vulnerability it can also serve as a creative resource for intervention for eliminating sexual harassment. Many traditional cultures have mechanisms like public shaming or community healing that can be mobilized as resources to confront gender-based violence generally and sexual harassment specifically.

Victim Blaming

One issue that follows on the question of the role male power plays in sexual harassment as well as cultural notions of sexually appropriate behaviour has to do with victim blaming. On several occasions, the cause of being sexually-harassed has been placed squarely on women's shoulders. Kelly (1988), in discussing the ideological processes through which women are blamed for men's violence, notes that men view women as sexual commodities and sex with a woman as a male entitlement. She utilizes the concept *sexual access* (a range of processes through which women are defined as sexual objects available only to men) to explain further how women get blamed for their sexually harassing experiences. She explains that feminists apply this concept in two related contexts. First, men sexualize all relationships with women and in so doing assume sexual access to women not known or slightly known to them. Men thus see sex as a male entitlement. Secondly, sexual access within the context of intimate relationships, like other resources, is determined by relational power. The more power a man can claim over a particular woman the greater his claim to exclusive access. The greater his perceived right to exclusive sexual access, the more likely it is that some level of sexual aggression will be considered legitimate (Kelly, 1988).

Koss and Cleveland (1997) note that the notion of the "deserving victim" provides justification for male sexual aggression. Women are expected to change their behaviour in order to bring the problem under control. The responsibility for women's safety is often placed on their shoulders. They are often blamed for provoking sexual harassment by their appearance, mode of dressing, by being in the wrong place at the wrong time, leading on their harassers or by having a history or being in a situation that makes them prone to be sexually-harassed (Kelly 1988; Twumasi, 2002). A keen debate rages on Ghanaian university campuses on how female dressing provokes sexually-harassing behaviours in males and promotes other forms of sexual violence against women. In 2001, students of the University of Ghana undertook a demonstration to protest against the provocative dressing of females and how this particular mode of dressing leads to sexual harassment (*Daily Graphic,* October 2001).

Women internalize this ideology and use it to control their sexual impulses and desires. Such women are more likely to assign greater responsibility to female victims including themselves for incidents of sexual harassment (Jasen and Gutek, 1982; Heise *et al.,* 1995). Avoidance behaviour is one form of expression that the internalization of blame on the part of women takes. The end result is the classification of women as justifiable recipients of unwanted sex, an overt permission to sexually-aggressive men to view their actions against women "not as extreme or unacceptable, but part of and consistent with 'normal' behaviour. With this permission, it is understandable that sexually-aggressive men are more likely to be proud of their coercive behaviours than ashamed or guilty" (Koss and Cleveland, 1997).

Victim blaming is a powerful reminder of male privilege. The traditional sex role stereotypes from which it flows allows males more freedom in expressing their sexuality. Victim blaming is often used to justify women's need for a restricted but supposedly safe space and highly-controlled sexual expression. The social environment which supports victim blaming creates a strong disincentive for women and girls to report their experience of violence to the authorities for justice (Koss and Cleveland, 1997; Fiscian *et al.,* 2003). Females internalize the principles that justify male violence and feel that they asked for it. The system tends to stigmatize sexual harassment victims. The general lack of information coupled with delayed justice creates a situation where many females do not see any returns for reporting their experience of harassment.

Causes of Sexual Harassment

Research has tried to locate the cause of sexual harassment as part of efforts to prevent or eliminate its occurrence at work and in academic institutions. Some have looked for personality factors; others have looked to norms and practices within the community or society and attempted to isolate peculiar personal or social characteristics at the centre of sexual harassment. Dall'Ara and Maass (1999), for example, looked at factors that facilitate or inhibit sexual harassment and stressed that sexual harassment is unlikely to occur unless there is a specific constellation of personality and situational variables conducive to such a behaviour. Their conclusion was that it is not a question of a particular personality type with the predisposition to harass but rather a total absence of normative standards prohibiting sexual harassment.

The local normative context within the organization has emerged as an important predicator of sexual harassment (i.e. system response). Work settings can be considered at risk when they are traditionally male dominated or when they make sexual abuse easy (Dall'Ara and Maass, 1999). In their work on date rape amongst university students, Koss and Cleveland (1997) note that sexual aggression is consistent with and supported by a dominant cultural understanding of sexual relations that endorses sexual coercion. Sexually aggressive men seek environments that are supportive of their pre-existing beliefs and past behaviours towards women. Fiscian *et al.*, (2003) make a similar observation when they note that schools in Ghana and Malawi are breeding grounds for potentially-damaging gendered practices. The prevalence of sexual aggression and the dominant male behaviour which supports it go largely unpunished creating the impression that abusive behaviour against females is normal and acceptable (Fiscian *et al.*, 2003).

Research by the University of Cape Town (1991), as well as by Hughes and Sandler (1988) who studied peer harassment in colleges in the United States, identified conditions most likely to promote the occurrence of sexual harassment as in situations where males outnumber females and especially where "alcohol is present, the incidence of harassment is more likely to occur" (Hughes and Sandler, 1988: 7). Other conditions identified were community tolerance, attitudes that ignore, or condone sexually-harassing events, which were said to send the message that some members of the community can be treated with disdain and lack of respect or even violence. University "traditions" and student organizations where victims at the receiving end "inadvertently" participate in their own victimization were some of the causes they mentioned.

In looking at personality factors, Dall'Ara and Maass (1999) describe the concept *likelihood to sexually harass* (LSH) and the corresponding scale developed by Pryor. They note that studies on LSH have shown that men with high scores tend to have a marked inclination toward sexual violence to identify themselves with hyper masculine gender-role stereotypes and to describe their behaviour as caused by a desire for domination. Men with high LSH tend to adopt behaviours in sexual situations that facilitate harassment.

Koss and Cleveland (1997) conclude that a sexually-coercive

environment is finally a web of mutually-dependent relationships between male behaviour, female responses, societal reactions, peer support and system response. Personality factors that predisposes individuals to sexually harass are socially derived; they are not biologically determined. Ideas about gender roles and strong desire to dominate women are derived from the specific social settings that carve out male notions of masculinity. Sexual harassment is, therefore, environment bound; no matter an individual's propensity to harass a non-permissive environment will act as an effective deterrent.

Sexual Harassment in Ghana

In Ghana, sexual harassment is believed to be pervasive even though there are very few reported cases. To date, the only well-known and recorded investigation on sexual harassment is that by CHRAJ in the case where Professor Frank Norvor was found guilty of sexually-harassing his employee, a flight attendant (*Public Agenda,* 1999). Ghanaian women who are sexually-harassed do not report their experiences for several reasons[12]. In the first place, several victims of sexual harassment are not aware of the fact that sexual harassment is against Ghanaian law. Secondly, there are the unacknowledged victims who do not know that their experiences constitute sexual harassment[13]. Most respondents in a sexual harassment study in Ghana conducted by Bortei-Doku Aryeetey (2004) had become conscious of the offensive nature of sexual harassment only in the last ten years. She blames factors such as a general lack of consensus on the degree of offence caused by certain types of behaviours, a lack of agreement as to who should take responsibility for causing the offence and a general tendency to confuse such acts with so-called normal sexual overtures for this delayed awakening. The cultural environment in Ghana discourages females from reporting their sexual harassment experiences because of the belief that a good and well-brought-up woman does not make public issues that hinge on her sexuality. Finally, the absence of well-defined structures for receiving complaints place victims at loss as to how to pursue justice to end their harassing experiences (*Tete-Mensah 2003).*

Studies such as those by Coker-Appiah and Cusack (1999), Fiscian *et al.,* (2003) and AWLA (2003) conclude that sexual harassment exists within a variety of contexts in Ghana. Coker-Appiah and Cusack (1999) reveal that both adolescent girls and women have suffered some forms of sexual harassment in their lives. Fiscian, Leach and Casely-Hayford discovered wide-ranging forms of sexual harassment in Ghanaian basic schools. Girls their research revealed suffered sexual harassment from their teachers and male colleagues. There existed in these basic schools situations where female pupils were trading sexual favours for money and other material goods, marks and promotion to the higher classes. The AWLA Ghana (2003) study showed that 63 per cent of respondents had experienced some forms sexual harassment at the workplace or within educational institutions. Major forms included comments on physical appearance (33 per cent), repeated requests for dates and unwanted touching (27 per cent each) and gender-based insults. The harassers in the AWLA Ghana (2003) study were mainly male colleagues or superiors of their female victims.

Sexual harassment constitutes an offence within Ghanaian law. There is, however, no legal provision designed specifically to offer redress to all victims of sexual harassment. A few legal provisions exist that can be utilized in Ghana to seek legal remedy. These include the Labour Act (Act 651) passed in July 2003 and before it, the Industrial Relations Act of 1962 and the Criminal Code (Amendment) Act 1998 (Act 554). Similar provisions can be found in the 1992 Ghanaian Constitution and the CHRAJ Act (Act 456). In giving judgement in the first case of sexual harassment ever to be arbitrated in Ghana, the Commissioner for Human Rights and Administrative Justice explained that the 1992 Constitution of Ghana and the CHRAJ Act, Act 456 give the Commission the jurisdiction to investigate complaints alleging sex discrimination and or violation of human rights (*Public Agenda,* 1999). Sexual harassment, according to the Commissioner, amounts to sex discrimination and a violation of human rights under Ghanaian law.

The Labour Act (Act 651) which was passed in 2003 brought together all Ghanaian labour laws, makes sexual harassment an offence. It defines sexual harassment as ". . . any unwelcome offensive or importunate sexual advance or request made by an employer or superior officer or a co-worker to a worker whether the worker is a man or a woman" (Part XX Section 173). Under this Act, a worker can terminate an employment contract on the grounds of unfair treatment or sexual harassment (*see* part III section 15b). Under unfair termination of employment, the Labour Act states in Part VIII section 63 that ". . . a worker's employment is deemed to be unfairly terminated . . . because the employer has failed to take action on repeated complaints of sexual harassment of the worker at the workplace". Such a worker can make a formal complaint to the labour commission and if the investigation of the commission concludes that the worker's appointment has been unfairly terminated then the law provides the following remedies:

1. Re-instatement of the worker from the date of the termination of employment;
2. Re-employment of the worker either in the work where the worker was employed before the termination or in other reasonably suitable work on the same terms and conditions enjoyed by the worker before the termination;
3. Payment of compensation to the worker (Part VIII section 64).

The remedies awarded by CHRAJ in the first case of sexual harassment ever to be arbitrated in Ghana went further than the provisions embodied in the Labour Act outlined above. The harasser Frank Norvor was ordered to pay monetary compensation to the victim. The monetary compensation was for injury to dignity, damaged feelings and self respect or humiliation in addition to loss of salary from wrongful termination of appointment plus interest at the going bank rate. The harasser was also ordered to cease the harassing conduct and to refrain from committing similar or same violation. CHRAJ considered factors such as the nature of the harassment, the degree of aggressiveness, and physical contact, the time periods and frequency with which the behaviour was experienced, the vulnerability of the victim and finally the psychological impact of the harassment on the victim in making awards.

The absence of a specific legal provision to which people who suffer sexual harassment can have recourse can be limiting despite the existence of all these legal provisions in Ghana at the moment. Under the Labour Act (Act 651), one can seek redress, only if sexual harassment is experienced in the workplace. In fact, the definition supplied by the law even restricts the occurrence of sexual harassment to the workplace and to behaviours on the part of the employer or the superior officer (see Part XX Section 173 of the Labour Act). Even though the provisions in the Act constitute significant achievements in the legal struggle for redress against sexual harassment, they are restricted in their application and therefore do not cover the experiences of students within educational institutions for example. Reddi (2003) explains, whilst reviewing the legal remedies on sexual harassment available under South African law, that the provisions that cover employment relations and restricts the experience of sexual harassment to the workplace excludes large groups of employees and other members of the general public. She explains, for example, that persons applying for employment are merely potential employees, clients and customers definitely are not employees and as such cannot be covered by the provisions in the labour law.

The provisions offered by the criminal law for seeking redress for having suffered sexual harassment have their limitations too. Reddi, still examining the South African situation, explains that ". . . criminal law appears to be a rather blunt instrument, ill-designed to deal with the problems of sexual harassment" (Reddi, 2003). The problems arise from the heavy burden of proof in criminal investigations where the prosecution has to prove beyond reasonable doubt that the criminal charge occurred. In several instances sexual harassment experiences were likely to have occurred behind closed doors and the testimony of the victim ". . . is quite likely to be regarded as uncorroborated evidence" (Reddi, 2003). Other drawbacks in pursuing justice using the criminal law for sexual harassment derive from the publicity that such a case might attract and the threat to the continuing employment of victims who are in active employment; or to their future employment prospects. Laws on sexual harassment in several instances recognize this problem and require victims to establish only a *prima facie* case of sexual harassment. The onus shifts to the accused to disprove the accusation.

These limitations point to the need for a sexual harassment specific legal provision in Ghana that offers victims proper legal facilities for redress. AWLA Ghana's efforts in this direction should provide a useful policy for the workplace (AWLA Ghana, 2003). The peculiar nature of educational settings, however, will have to be addressed with more specific provisions. In the chapters that follow, we discuss our findings from the field within the framework of the explanations outlined here and determine the extent to which conditions in Ghanaian universities compare to the situation in other places where the debate on sexual harassment is well advanced.

Chapter 3

PERCEPTIONS AND ATTITUDES TO SEXUAL HARASSMENT

Introduction

An effective policy on sexual harassment will have to take into account the target community's assumptions, attitudes and beliefs as well as their perceptions. People's perceptions of any social issue determines, to a large extent, how they process information they receive about the event and their subsequent reactions to it. The assumptions that people have of sexual harassment, determine their understanding of the likely causes and impact. Information on perceptions and attitudes that feed sexual harassment becomes crucial for outlining what the final content and focus of the preventive measures that a sexual harassment policy for a university institution should cover. This chapter starts with a description of the background of respondents and follows with an examination of the definition of sexual harassment on the various campuses. There is also an attempt to signal the variations in perceptions that exist amongst the various sections of the university community.

The Respondents

An examination of the age and marital status of respondents, as to be expected, shows that student respondents tend to be the youngest and teaching staff the oldest. For example, nearly 46 per cent of teaching staff were within the age range of 41–60 years, one third of non-teaching staff were 45 years and above, and about 9 per cent of students were above 40 years (Fig 3.1). Over 57 per cent of the student respondents were 30 years and below, the proportion of teaching and non-teaching staff respondents who fell within this age group was 14 per cent and 32 per cent respectively.

Student respondents tend to be single and had never been married (80 per cent); most of the teaching and non-teaching staff respondents, on the other hand, were married. The proportion of teaching staff respondents that were married was higher than the non-teaching staff

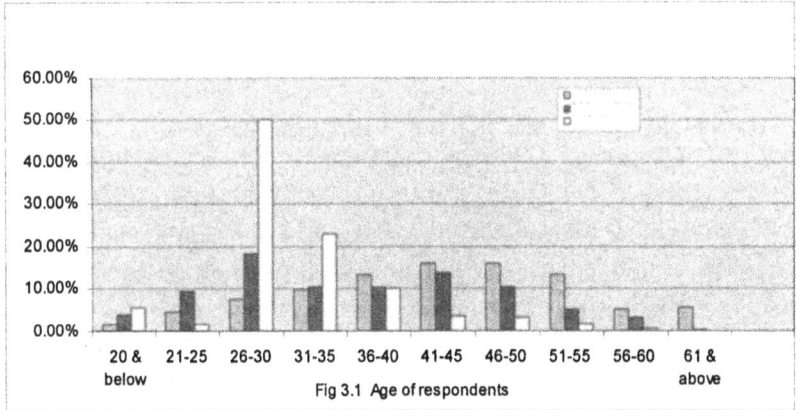

Fig 3.1 Age of respondents

respondents (72 per cent as against 58 per cent). Though very few respondents fell within the other categories of marital status of divorced, widowed, separated and consensual relationships, the proportion of non-teaching staff respondents in these groups was highest. Age may explain why more teaching staff respondents were married than the others but it does not explain why non-teaching staff had the highest proportion of the divorced or those living in consensual relationship (Fig 3.2). Further investigations might provide useful insights to such variations in marital status for non-teaching and teaching staff.

Respondents tend to be engaged in religious activities both on and

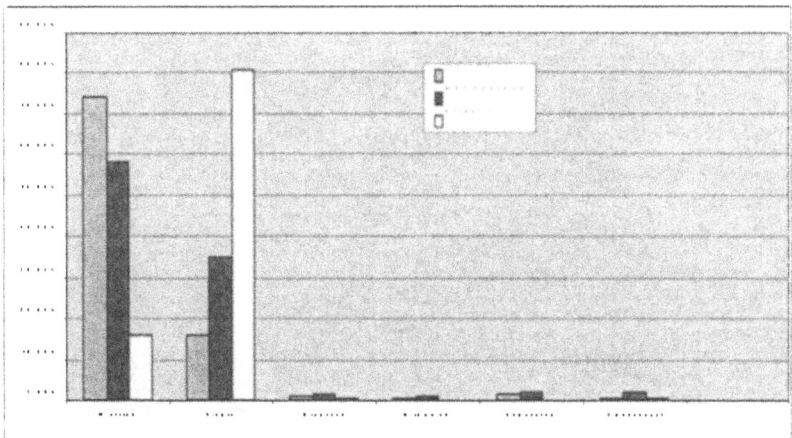

Fig 3.2 Marital status of respondents

off the university campuses. In fact, more teaching and non-teaching staff respondents were active in off-campus religious activities than they were in on-campus groups (*see* Figs 3.3a and 3.3b). Students, on the other hand were active in on-campus religious activities. Teaching staff were more involved in social and professional activities than students and non-teaching staff off-campus. Non-teaching staff respondents' involvement in non-religious grouping both on and off-campus was lowest. The female/male analysis of participation in groupings reveals only a slight difference in terms of participation in both on-campus and off-campus activities. More female teaching staff participate regularly in professional activities than males. Male respondents are more involved in social and political groupings than females. More females reported being involved in religious activities on campus than males. More males over 40 per cent were, however, in academic groupings on campus than females (a little over 30 per cent).

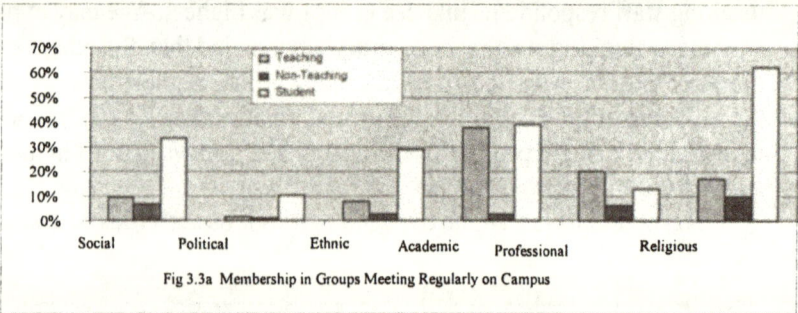

Fig 3.3a Membership in Groups Meeting Regularly on Campus

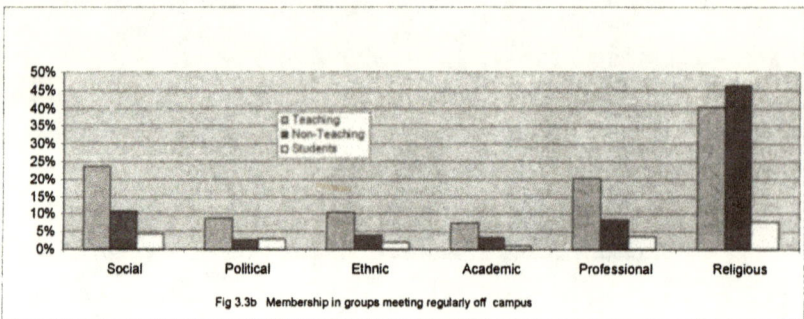

Fig 3.3b Membership in groups meeting regularly off campus

Naming Sexual Harassment

One key area in any policy on sexual harassment is how it will define sexual harassment and what behaviours will be categorized as actionable. Our discussion on the definition of sexual harassment confirmed the caution of Reilly, *et al;* (1999) about the need for clarity in the definition of sexual harassment on which policies depend. This section explores how respondents on the university campuses define sexual harassment as well as the events they label sexually-harassing. Attempts are made, where possible, to discern any possible differences in terms of how the sex of respondents might influence their perceptions, reactions, attitudes and beliefs.

Literature on the definition of sexual harassment discussed earlier notes that three main elements feature in the numerous definitions offered (Aeberhard-Hodges, 1997). These are the perceptions of the one at the receiving end, the intention of the harasser and the impact of the action whether or not it violates the rights of the harassed, and/or demeans or causes injury both physical and emotional. For respondents on the university campuses it was the sexual intention of the act that qualifies it as sexual harassment. Most definitions offered made reference to the sexual nature of the act.

Respondents' expressions of their understanding of sexual harassment were spelt out as:

1. Verbal sexual remarks or jokes;
2. Gestures, demand and subtle pressures for sex;
3. Behaviours that have sexual connotations directed at eliciting sexual reactions;
4. Physical contacts with the opposite sex;
5. Sexual intercourse in return for a favour;
6. Sexual assault.

A few gave definitions that looked at the impact and stated that sexual harassment consisted of actions that are designed to create distress in someone about his/her sexual activities. Some were explicit that the behaviours targeted women. The range of definitions classified as sexual harassment by non-teaching staff respondents was wider than for the other groups. The non-teaching staff respondents identified extra marital relations amongst university staff and acts by males to undermine females in the workplace as sexual harassment (Table 3.1). Extra marital sexual relations present a challenge when it occurs between members of the university community with unequal institutional power and status especially if the male happens to be in position of authority. The debate centres on the point at which such a relationship becomes an avenue for sexual favouritism and corruption, a tool for peddling academic and occupational favours in exchange for sex. Relationships of this nature cannot be free from some form of coercion. Group discussion sessions posed this as a dilemma and raised questions about how free such relations will be of personal gain.

TABLE 3.1

Defining Sexual Harassment

Definition	Students (%)			Teaching Staff (%)			Non-Teaching Staff (%)		
	Female	Male	All	Female	Male	All	Female	Male	All
Subtle pressure/ gestures for sex	44.7	43.6	44.1	39.7	41.3	40.5	29.1	29.8	29.4
Forced sex/rape	9.5	8.5	9.1	1.4	8.4	6	12.2	18.2	15.1
Arouse sexual feelings	12.3	18.9	15.3	8.2	7.7	8.3	11.8	11.6	11.7
Uninvited physical contact with opposite sex	9.6	7.5	8.6	16.4	8.4	11.1	8.4	5.3	6.9
Demand for sexual favours under veiled threats	2.8	5.3	3.9	8.2	8.4	8.3	4.6	8.9	6.7
Offensive sexual jokes	4.4	5.7	5	5.5	0.7	2.3	6.8	1.8	4.3
Use of power to demand sexual favours	0	0	0	5.5	4.9	5.1	1.7	2.2	1.9
Jokes about sex to females	1.2	0.9	1.1	1.4	2.1	1.8	0.8	1.3	1.1
Extra marital sex	0	0	0	0	0	0	0.8	0.4	0.6
Males undermine women	0	0	0	0	0	0	0.4	0	0.2
No response/No idea/Can't tell	15.5	9.6	12.9	13.7	18.1	16.6	23.4	20.5	22.1
Total	100	100	100	100	100	100	100	100	100

Source: Field Data: 2001.
Workshop definitions covered the subjective interpretation of the harassed and the key words supplied included "unwanted" or "unwelcome" and the fact that the action should be gender-based. The subjective nature of the act was not given much prominence by respondents. What was important is the intention of the act and its content, whether it is sexual or not. Sex, therefore, appears to play a role in the definition of sexual harassment on all the university campuses (Table 3.1). One problematic area was the definition that specified sexual harassment as actions which stimulate emotions. The danger pointed out was that too many actions can be covered by this and there is the risk of failing to offer protection to the real victims of sexual harassment. Not all actions that stimulate emotions are sexually-harassing and on the other hand not all sexually-harassing behaviours stimulate emotions. More females than males in all categories felt that unwanted sexual contact with the opposite sex was sexually harassing.

3.4 Behaviours Classified as Sexual Harassment

In our discussions in the second chapter on how sexual harassment is categorized we noted that Dall'Ara and Maass (1999) and Henry and Meltzoff (1998) group sexually-harassing behaviours into two; those that create a hostile environment and those involving sexual coercion. The present study found a group of behaviours classified by respondents as sexual harassment that could not all fit into any of these two groups. These behaviours were, therefore, classified as sexual provocation.

Behaviours respondents identified as sexual harassment included male behaviour directed at females to make them feel uncomfortable, threatened or demeaned thus creating a hostile environment. These were:

1. Unwanted physical contact (most cited behaviour) (40 per cent);
2. Suggestive looks and remarks (13 per cent);
3. Exposure to pornographic materials, (1 per cent).

More female respondents in all categories felt that unwanted sexual contact with the opposite sex was sexually-harassing.

The second group of behaviours identified by respondents as sexually-harassing were sexually coercive in nature (Table 3.2). These were:

1. Demand for sex under a veiled threat in exchange for some academic or occupational benefit (sexual bribery) (14 per cent);
2. Forced sex or rape (1 per cent).

TABLE 3.2

Behaviours Classified as Sexual Harassment

Sexually Harassing Behaviours	Students (%)			Non-Teaching Staff (%)			Teaching Staff (%)		
	Female	Male	All	Female	Male	All	Female	Male	All
Uninvited physical contact	52	36.1	44.8	35.6	17.8	26.6	38.4	35	35.9
Demand/pressure for sex under threat	9.6	18.1	13.5	14.3	20.9	17.5	19.2	9.1	12.9
Suggestive looks/ remarks/gestures	10.7	12.2	11.4	12.2	20	16	5.5	16.8	12.9
Provocative dressing	7.4	17.5	12	3.8	8.9	6.3	6.8	9.8	8.8
Exposure to pornography	0.5	1.1	0.8	0.4	0.4	0.4	0	0.7	0.5
Unwanted visit/ Attention	1.1	1	1.1	0.4	4	4	0	1.4	1
Sexual discrimination	0	0	0	0.4	4	4	1.4	1.4	1.4
Improper sitting postures	0.4	1.1	0.7	0	0.4	0.2	0	0	–
Body language during conversation	0.9	1.4	1.1	1.7	2.7	2.2	0	0	–
Demand for favours/ Gifts	0.5	0.9	0.7	3	2.7	2.8	2.7	1.4	1.8
Intimidation/Threats	0	0	0	0.8	2.5	1.6	0	2.1	1.4
Forced sex/Rape	0.5	0.3	0.4	0	0	0	0	0	0
Not filled/No response	16.4	10.3	13.5	27.4	15.7	18.4	26	22.3	23.4
Total	100	100	100	100	100	100	100	100	100

Source:　Field Data: 2001.

The list of behaviours outlined as actionable at the workshops, on the other hand, was similar to those highlighted in the research finding.

The behaviours were those that fell under:
1. Hostile environment, like:
    i. Verbal — unacceptable comments, insults, whistling cat-calls, sexual discussion, group daunting and teasing;
    ii. Non-verbal actions — suggestive gestures, staring, suggestive smiles, cartooning and lampooning on student media, voyeurism;
    iii. Unwanted physical contact, touching, fondling, and kissing.

2. Sexual coercion:
    i. Rape;
    ii. Sexual favouritism and sexual bribery through gifts in return for sexual favours

The third group of behaviours identified by respondents and workshop participants which we have termed sexual provocation were mainly female behaviours that were said to sexually-harass males. The first set included behaviours that had the tendency to arouse males sexually. Certain actions on the part of females like the way they dress were noted by respondents to stimulate in males an urge for sex and as such were sexually-harassing. The response of a male student in a group interview session explains this attitude:

> I think to some extent dressing also influences these things. . . . Sometimes, I see a lady who is dressed in a certain way. Suddenly, I have an interest in the lady.

The second set covered gestures and behaviours on the part of females interpreted by males as invitation for sex, for example:

    i. Female student visiting her male colleague at what is described as an odd hour;
    ii. Female student sitting on the bed of a male colleague she has gone to visit;
    iii. "Improper sitting posture";
    iv. "Body language";
    v. Request for lunch date or an outing;
    vi. Request for academic support.

The behaviours listed above were interpreted by the males to be an invitation to have sex and if the males are not ready for sex then it becomes sexual harassment. For males, actions and behaviours on the part of the females which stimulate in them an urge for sex constitutes sexual harassment.

We see at play here what Kelly (1988) identifies as the notion of male entitlement. For her, men tend to sexualize their relations with women and see them as sexual commodities. Thus, whatever women do in the presence of men is subject to a sexual interpretation whether or not they are asking for sex. This notion was not exclusively the perception of males alone. It was shared to a large extent by females as well (Table 3.2).

Other behaviours cited as constituting harassment are female demands for academic or occupational support. Such needs are important for personal, professional or academic advancement of females on the university campus. Other demands cover a request for a lunch, date or an outing demands form females suggest that they are putting up an invitation for sex. Demands for favours from females suggest that they (the females) are ready to return the favour with sex. The perception was that females understand that nothing can be obtained free, and once a male does a favour that a female accepts, she has implicitly agreed to pay back with sex. Favours such as dating for example should be paid back. When a female persistently makes such demands of a male, then she is subjecting him to sexual harassment if he has no sexual interest in her.

The workshops identified yet another form of sexually-harassing behaviour termed offensive sexual conduct. This included behaviours that were generally conceived as inappropriate, morally-incorrect or offensive sexual behaviour. An example cited was students having sex in the presence of their roommates.

The perception that female dressing can provoke sexual harassment and that some females dress to provoke sexual reaction in males is not limited to Ghana. Studying the perceptions of sexual harassment on the campus of the College of Education at Ilorin in Nigeria, Dawene (1985) identified sexual harassment as the outcome of morally-decadent females attempt to satisfy a huge appetite for material wealth. He quotes several sources to show that female students deliberately dress to seduce male lecturers for two reasons. First, female students spend time on non-academic activities during school sessions and in their efforts to make up for lost time they become easy prey for sexual harassers (Dawene, 1985). Secondly, female students who are academically weak succumb to harassment pressures from lecturers in return for covering up their weaknesses. Females offer their bodies any time they seek favours from males. He concludes by stating that the fact that a few female students are ready to sell their bodies for favours is no excuse for any lecturer to sexually-harass these girls (*ibid*). Male perceptions of female sexuality become key component in identifying sexually harassing behaviours. The muplications of such perceptions for identifying actionable behaviour is discussed later.

The nature of the experience alone is inadequate in trying to recognize and label sexually-harassing experiences because certain circumstances can render a behaviour normally classified as sexual harassment more tolerable and therefore wanted. The form the harassment takes is important because some verbal forms are so subtle that the onus falls on the harassed to complain at the risk of appearing paranoid or fussy. This personal testimony of a female student respondent best illustrates the point:

> Listen and imagine this situation. You're working in a group and you ask, "So how do we start answering the question?" Then a man will get up and say "Before we answer this question, I think we should weave around the question and finally penetrate". Then he'll be staring at you. Do you get what I mean? It is so uncomfortable using suggestive language. Yes the next moment, you are speaking and say, "It was under it" then he looks at you and says, "Is that your normal position? Do you always go under it? Hmm?" Then the third one, he will touch you like to say "Good morning" then, he will say "Does that give you ideas about the kind of things that have been happening?" The same person, so what do you do?

In this case, the female feels clearly harassed and asks appropriately what one can do in such a circumstance; for her, reporting to an institutional authority is too harsh and yet she will want the experience to end.

The source of the behaviour, according to respondents, also determines whether it was sexual harassment or not. Certain actions by a student to a fellow student were not considered sexually harassing. Female student respondents found it awkward for lecturers to touch them but would tolerate such behaviour from their male peers. The marital status of a victim appeared to be a factor in determining whether an experience should be classified as sexual harassment. Respondents appeared more sympathetic towards married women who experience sexual harassment. Thus, a little over half of all respondents found it a serious violation of rights if a married woman should suffer sexual harassment.

TABLE 3.3

Respondents Who Think That Sexual Harassment is a Serious Violation of the Rights of Certain Victims

Type of Victim	Non-Teaching staff				Teaching staff				All			
	Females		Males		Female		Male		Female		Male	
	No	%	No	%	No	%	No	%	No	%	No	%
Married woman	124	52.3	125	55.6	44	60.3	66	45.8	168	56.1	191	51.8
Unmarried woman	33	13.9	32	14.2	19	26.0	44	30.6	52	19	76	20.6
Married man	20	8.4	20	8.9	10	13.7	30	20.8	30	11	50	13.6
Others	60	25.4	48	21.3	0	0	4	2.8	60	13.9	52	14.0
Total	237	100	225	100	73	100	144	100	310	100	369	100

Source: Field Data: 2001.

About 14 per cent felt the same way when it was a married man who experienced the sexual harassment. More respondents felt that it was more serious for a married woman than an unmarried woman to experience sexual harassment (Table 3.3). Respondents' reasons for this assertion were varied, the list below summarizes the reasons given.

1.   Just not right /fornication morally wrong;
2.   Religiously not right/against the will of God;
3.   Culturally unacceptable;
4.   Abstinence is the best;
5.   Society frowns on that;
6.   Can lead to sexual harassment.

Not all behaviours normally classified as sexual harassment are accepted by everyone for two reasons. The harasser does not see the action as sexually-harassing, and in other instances, the harassed does not recognize the event as sexual harassment. There appears to be some agreement as to what constitutes sexual harassment amongst respondents. The nature of an event alone is not sufficient to qualify it as a sexually harassing act. Circumstances such as the source of the event and the manner in which the harasser and the harassed view the event were identified as key factors. In addition, respondents believed that the seriousness of a sexually harassing experience is determined by the marital status of the harassed.

There were some diffences between the student and staff respondents in terms of whether or not women enjoy sexually-harassing events. Whilst 54 per cent of all student respondents agreed that sexually-harassing events do not offend all females and that some even enjoy them, about one quarter of non-teaching staff respondents believed that some women enjoy sexually-harassing events. The proportion for teaching staff respondents was lower, and fewer female teaching staff (14 per cent) than male teaching staff (22 per cent) believed that women enjoy being sexually harassed as this statement from a male respondent at a group discussion session reveals:

> "females themselves don't think it is harassment in that context because they have come [to] have fun with them".

For some respondents sexual harassment charges are exaggerations on the part of females and others make up stories about being sexually harassed. More male students tend to hold this view. Nearly 70 per cent males, as against, 30 per cent female teaching staff thought that sexual harassment charges were mere exaggerations. About one-half of male non-teaching staff agreed to this assertion as against 40 per cent of their female counterparts.

Developing a definition of sexual harassment on university campuses in Ghana on which to base a policy faces some challenges. Definitions of sexual harassment determine which behaviour should be labelled as sexual harassment and should attract sanctions. Plenary sessions of the dissemination workshops were characterized by debates over sexuality, sexual morality and sexually-appropriate behaviours. There is the danger that confusion about sexual morality might lead to a loose definition. The observations of the workshops should, however, offer some guidelines. The workshops, for example, noted the need to find ways to criminalize sexual harassment by locating injury to human dignity within it. In this way, sexual harassment will cease to be a personal experience that happens to females who are morally loose.

There are several reasons why a definition of sexual harassment should be accurate and in addition acknowledge the potential harm on victims. Bortei-Doku Aryeetey (2004) cautions that prolonged arguments about ambiguity in the definition of sexual harassment and circumstances leading to it can be misleading and serve to dilute the seriousness attached to this behaviour. In her workshop presentation, Tete-Mensah quoting Crocker and Rice, suggested that sexual harassment definitions should be accurate for two main reasons.

> In the first place, sexual harassment within the workplace is a spill over of traditional gender perceptions that operate in homes to the work situations
> Secondly, occupational sex segregation make women easy victims of sexual harassment because hierarchical structures within organizations provide "opportunity structures" enabling male occupants of positions of authority to use legitimate power to compel persons of lower status to interact with them sexually.

An accurate definition provides a framework for educating the entire university community on the implications of sexual harassment. For victims, sexual harassment provides legal ammunition in the pursuit of justice. Finally, since sexual harassment is the direct outcome of gendered interactions a good definition enables organizations deal better with other gender related issues.

Setting Tolerance Levels for Sexual Harassment

The level of tolerance of people to social problems is a critical factor in any attempt to deal with the problem: how people view the problem influences what levels they are ready to tolerate. Levels of tolerance also help to determine how visible the problem is in a community or culture. Respondents were asked to respond to situations by indicating

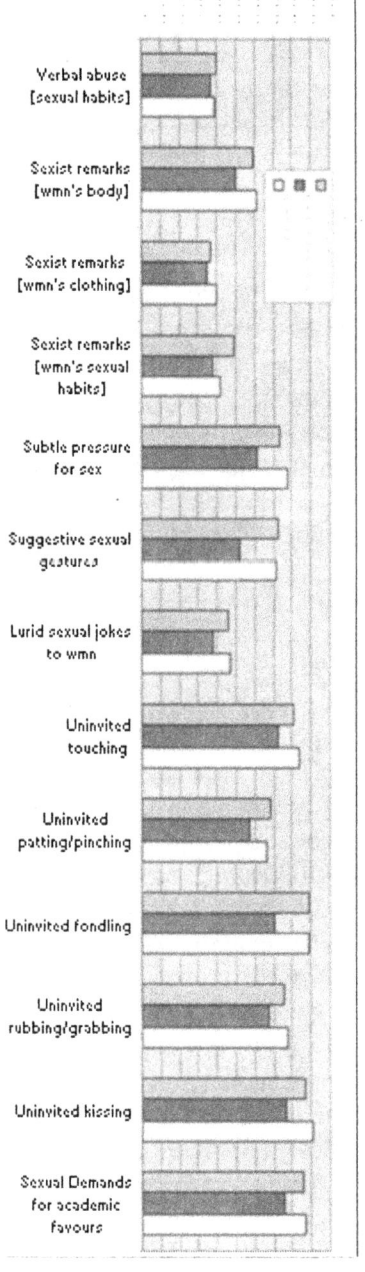

Fig 3.4a Proportion of respondents finding harassing conditions unacceptable

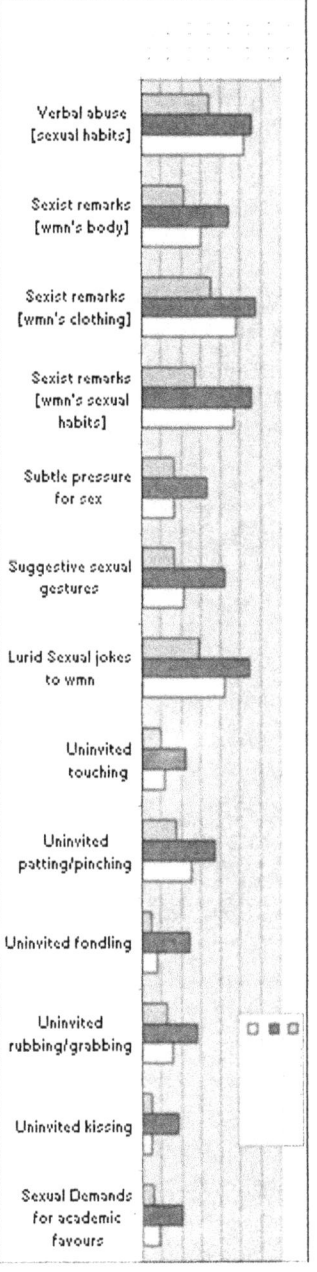

Fig 3.4b Proportion of respondents finding harassing conditions acceptable

whether they agree or disagree to certain sexually-harassing situations. The results of their reactions are presented in Fig 3.4a and 3.4b. On the whole it appears that there are some patterns in the tolerance levels of the three groups of respondents: teaching, non-teaching and students. Teaching staff and student respondents were less tolerant of sexual harassment behaviours than non-teaching staff respondents.

The perceptions of the teaching staff respondents about sexually-harassing situations shows a sex difference in what respondents are likely to find acceptable. Females were more intolerant than males. Respondents appeared to be more tolerant of gestures and verbal comments than they were of physical contacts (Fig 3.4a and 3.4b). Thus, the proportion of respondents who found situations like verbal abuse, lurid jokes, and sexist remarks about a woman's clothing or sexual habits acceptable was higher than those who did not. Most respondents saw physical contact or behaviours with a clear connotation of sex as unacceptable. Situations like subtle pressure for sex and demands for sex for most respondents were unacceptable, so were situations that call for physical contact like uninvited kissing, fondling, patting/pinching or touching.

Perceptions about Possible Triggers of Sexual Harassment

This section examines the conditions that respondents identified as possible triggers of sexual harassment as well as the members of the university community most likely to suffer sexual harassment. Most respondents (students 83 per cent, non-teaching staff 78 per cent and teaching staff 80 per cent) and likewise all workshops participants believed that more females than males suffer sexual harassment and as such females were more vulnerable. The most vulnerable female members identified were students and junior staff with the groups outlined below:

1. Fresh women;
2. Non-resident female students living in rented rooms of homes in communities surrounding the universities;
3. Academically-weak female students;
4. Female students who are needy financially;
5. Attractive female students;
6. Female secretaries.

Other vulnerable members identified were the high profile personalities like Deans and Heads of departments as well as female hawkers.

Respondents recognized female vulnerability and confirmed McKinnon's (1979) position that sexual harassment is the product of women's unequal status and that men have power over women and use that power to harass. Sexual harassment was the result of male sexualizing females and a further exploitation of unequal power relations by men. They also acknowledged the fact that male power is further buttressed by their ascribed institutional authority in the work or educational environment. Females are mainly harassed by males because they are more vulnerable. Men enjoy a higher social status than women and this gives them the advantage to use their positions to harass females in their place of work. Additionally, the fact that men culturally take the initiative to propose to women in all social encounters offers them an easy opening to harass. The sexual potential of a woman's body combined with her low status, makes her an easy victim of sexual harassment. About 10 per cent of respondents, however, believed that males have a stronger sexual desire than females and are, therefore, more likely to harass females. About 10 per cent of teaching staff, 15 per cent of non-teaching staff and 20 per cent of student respondents believed that females are harassed by males because female dressing harasses males who, in turn, feel provoked to harass females.

People believe that conditions surrounding academic issues were likely to attract sexual harassment. In terms of ranking the first four conditions were related to student academic work on the university campuses. Over 50 per cent of all respondents selected the following issues as the four most important conditions most likely to attract sexual harassment:

1. Good grade in examinations;
2. Passing end of semester examinations;
3. Basis for offering academic support;
4. Admission into programmes.

Most respondents believe that the pressure of academic work expose university students to sexual harassment. This raises questions about the conditions under which students carry out their academic work and the possible impact of sexual harassment or the threat of it on the way students conduct themselves whilst on campus. Respondents agreed that getting employment in the universities in which they worked was likely to provide an occasion to suffer sexual harassment. Here, though, there were differences of opinion within the sub groups of respondents. A higher proportion of non-teaching staff (35 per cent) than teaching staff (25 per cent) and students (20 per cent) agreed that getting a university appointment was likely to predispose one to sexual harassment. Fewer respondents agreed to the fact that work related conditions provide occasions for sexual harassment. What is interesting here is that about one in three non-teaching staff respondents believed that employment in the university was likely to attract sexually-harassing experience. A higher proportion of students (28 per cent) than university staff (22 per cent non-teaching and 17 per cent teaching) believed that promotion to higher ranks in the university provide a condition for sexual harassment.

Respondents generally believed that one's personality is an important factor in determining whether one will experience sexual harassment. In all instances over 50 per cent of respondents believed that personality traits such as the type of behaviour that one exhibits, mode of dressing, and ability to resist male advances influenced one's propensity to attract sexual harassment. Certain behaviours, especially from females, are seen as an invitation to men to have sex. A good number of respondents assumed that the way women present themselves, student respondents identified, as "body language", was an important factor contributing to sexual harassment. Over three quarters of all categories of respondents agreed that the way women presented themselves invites sexually-harassing behaviours from males. One notion that came up strongly was the fact that certain actions from females were an invitation to males to have sex as shown in this statement from a male respondent in one of the group interview sessions:

> All of the ladies come with pre-judged minds. But the man, most of the time, is carefree. It is very difficult for a woman who does not like you, who does not think of you, to come and decide to sit by you in the same place to share a mineral. A lot of girls would not even come here at all, they are just not interested. Others will come because they know what they will get. They themselves know

what will happen if they come to share the company of boys. I am going to this boy and this is what I want this boy to do. She is already determined to go and do that.

Male student respondents at group sessions expressed the opinion that failure to respond "appropriately" may be interpreted as a weakness. Thus, male students believed that they have to "prove that I am a man or risk ridicule."

"Provocative dressing" again is one such condition that was recorded by respondents as being responsible for attracting sexual harassment. The belief that the way people dress is the condition that triggers sexual harassment was pervasive on the university campus. The concern that this attitude raises is the level of sympathy that a female dressed in a manner considered "sexually provocative" will get from members of the university community should such a person suffer sexual harassment. Other related issues will be the tendency for people to dress or behave in a certain way if they believe that a particular behaviour can create conditions for attracting harassment. Clearly one can discern that the threat of experiencing a sexually-harassing event can circumscribe the behaviour of certain members of the university campuses. Bortei–Doku Aryeetey dismisses women's dress as legitimate grounds for attracting sex attacks and cautions that shifting the blame for harassment to dress habits seriously threatens women's right to freedom of expression, the right to decide what to wear. Dress as a trigger for sexual harassment for her amounts to victim blame selectively applied to women because the creativity of young men in transcending acceptable dress codes in Ghana has, on the whole, failed to generate the same level of public disapproval.

There was also the assumption that some types of programmes and even the names they carried encouraged sexual harassment. Students at a group discussion session stated that:

We have to sell the programmes that we organize on campus. The name of the programme is crucial. It entices them and pre-conditions their minds before they show up. There are names like "*bomeka*"[14] "*sosome so*"[15]. If you should go to such a place to "*bo*" somebody "*ka*" you should also think of what you give in return since nothing is free in today's Ghana. If you allow that person to spend on you, then you should also know what the stakes are for him.

Implied in the above statement is that nothing is free and once a female agrees to allow a male to spend money on her, she should be prepared to pay back and the mode of payment for males is sex. Sex here becomes the natural outcome for accepting favours from men and if women do not want to pay back, then they should not accept any favours from men. Such favours even extend to helping a student with her academic work. Females invite males to harass them sexually when they accept their gifts and favours. A female's presence at a particular place and time as well as her participation in certain events also encourage the assumption that she has come to be fondled otherwise she will not be there. Where women are and how they present themselves are always subject to interpretation by males about whether or not they are ready for sex. Earlier, these same behaviours had been identified as constituting in themselves sexual harassment. Here again, we find the "just cause" syndrome at play. The strong sentiment is not that females have transgressed some gender norms but rather interpretations of masculinity and what should be an appropriate male response to female behaviour. Responding 'appropriately' to female 'invitation' constitute essential feature in the determintion of masculinity for male university student.

Respondents acknowledged the fact that sexual harassment affects the way people behave. Nearly two thirds of all categories of respondents stated that some people behave in a certain way in order to avoid being sexually-harassed (77 per cent students, 62 per cent teaching staff and 62 per cent non-teaching staff). A higher proportion of students agreed to this assertion than teaching and non-teaching staff respondents. Between 37 per cent and 50 per cent of all respondents stated that females keep away from certain parts of the university campus in order to avoid being sexually harassed.

Another attitude discerned described sexual harassment as abnormal behaviour or people who sexually-harass others as abnormal. One quarter of staff respondents and one third of student respondents agreed to the assertion that sexual harassers act under the influence of some form of emotional or mental condition that makes them incapable of rational behaviour. One cannot say that a majority of respondents hold this view, yet the proportion is still substantial to warrant attention.

Female response to male advances and respondents' perception of

TABLE 3.4

Respondents' Perceptions about How to Interpret Females' Negative Response to Male Advances

Interpretation of female "No"	Students				Non-teaching staff				Teaching staff				All			
	F		M		F		M		F		M		F		M	
	No	%	No	%	No	%	No	%	No	%	No	%	No	%	No	%
No means "No"	439	56.4	167	25.9	104	43.9	58	26	47	64.4	61	42.7	590	54.2	286	28
No Means "Yes"	186	23.9	333	51.6	37	15.6	82	36	9	12.3	49	34.3	232	21.3	464	46
No Response/No Idea	154	19.7	146	22.5	96	40.5	85	38	17	23.3	34	23	267	24.5	265	26
Total	779	100	646	100	237	100	225	100	73	100	144	100	1089	100	1015	100

Source: Field Data: 2001

how females' response can be interpreted is one area that will require special attention in any sexual harassment policy. Female non-verbal cues were considered very important sexual harassment triggers for males. The study, therefore, investigated how female verbal response to male advances is perceived. Most males interpret female rejection of their sexual advances as an acceptance (about 46 per cent males). About one quarter of the male respondents agreed that a female "No" means "No" as against a little over half of the female respondents. Many more female teaching staff respondents (64 per cent) than male student and non-teaching staff respondents (26 per cent in both cases) affirmed that when females say "No" they really mean "No" (Table 3.4).

At the centre of the debate on sexual harassment is the thinking that females usually reject male advances for several reasons. First, it is seen as wrong for females to say "Yes" at the first instance to male advance. Such a female is seen as being promiscuous. Good and well-brought-up women do not give in to a male advance at the first try. Males themselves, therefore, do not expect females to say "Yes" on the first try. As a result they ignore any protestations from females to their (male) sexual advances. It is considered as not being masculine enough if a male gives up just because the female said "No" at a first try.

Shrinking university resources were also blamed as a possible cause of sexual harassment. Inadequate learning materials, poor infrastructure on campuses like the absence of street lights, limited accommodation facilities, increasing university fees push female students into the waiting hands of sexual harassers. A lecturer was suspended as result of corruption over student room allocation which he used as a bait for sexual favours[16]. Workshop reports noted that access to dwindling university resources are turned into tools for sexual exploitation of female students. Submission to sexual harassment can facilitate access to jobs or academic resources in some circumstances.

Contesting General Notions of Sexual Harassment Triggers

The notion that the way women dress or present themselves tends to provoke sexual harassment was contested at group discussion sessions on the various campuses and the dissemination workshops. Female respondents pointed out that some females also get sexually aroused when males expose themselves. According to one such respondent:

> Men think that it is only women who expose themselves, women also do get aroused and many get embarrassed on seeing men in half naked dresses and tight shorts, women do get excited.

People might have cause to complain about the way some women dress; all workshops concluded that female mode of dressing cannot constitute an accepted justification for sexual harassment. The question then is why male mode of dressing is not considered a possible source of sexual harassment. Can a female claim that she has been sexually-harassed by a male mode of dressing or even counter male "provocative dressing" with a sexually-harassing gesture and get societal nod as having acted appropriately? Some group sessions revealed that sections of the female members of the university communities were already avoiding researchers because they believed that the study was investigating the possibility of prescribing a uniform for female students to wear on the university campuses. Others felt that

> . . . a lot depends on the individual and what the individual is looking out for so if one is looking out for some women to invite him then a certain kind of behaviour will be interpreted as an invitation to harass.

For some student respondents especially females, this response at a group interview session best captures their attitude

> Behaviour can only be interpreted as an invitation to harass on the basis of how one sees things and not because that behaviour is itself an invitation.

The workshops concluded that the debate on mode of dressing can be used to divert attention from the real impact of sexual harassment. Blaming the occurrence of sexual harassment on the way females dress was simplistic and diversionary, the real issue at play on the university campuses were unequal gender relations. The workshops, therefore, pointed out the need to distinguish between sexual decency, sexually-inappropriate behaviours between mutually-consenting adults and sexual harassment as one of the first steps in developing a sexual harassment policy.

General Assumptions about Women

The study examined the general assumptions about women held by respondents on the university campuses. Here again, respondents were asked to indicate whether they agreed or disagreed with certain notions about women and their abilities in relation to work. Tables 3.5a and 3.5b capture the proportion of respondents who agreed with the notions presented below. The first table (Table 3.5a) covered gender stereotypes held by respondents and how these are likely to be transported into work relations. Only teaching and non-teaching staff were asked to respond to these assertions. Over 40 per cent of staff respondents agreed that notions about women held in the home were carried to the workplace. A higher proportion of teaching staff respondents agreed to these assertions than non-teaching staff respondents (54 per cent as against 45 per cent). About 40 per cent of respondents agreed that women should not lose sight of their gender status when dealing with men in the workplace. Fewer females than males agreed but the proportion of females who agreed was still high at about 36 per cent for female teaching staff as against nearly 47 per cent non-teaching staff. As a follow up with the earlier assertion, nearly one out of every two staff respondents believed that the gender position of women determined work relations in the universities. In this instance, a higher proportion of female teaching staff respondents (56 per cent) agreed than all the other category of respondents. Here again, the question is how far the perceptions reflect the truth or feeds into the reality and affects events.

Between 54 per cent and 60 per cent of staff respondents agreed that females were better at certain tasks than males; fewer agreed that females were only fit for certain positions in the university. There were differences in opinion and more non-teaching staff (about 15 per cent) than teaching staff (about 4 per cent) agreed. About three out of ten female teaching staff said they agreed to the fact that females are fit for certain positions only in the university. Between 6 per cent and 12 per cent of staff respondents agreed that females are not fit to hold headship positions in the universities because they can be easily manipulated by men (Table 3.5a).

In certain instances, respondents agreed that females and males are not the same and that gender relations feature prominently in work relations in the university. Most respondents; however, did not agree that

TABLE 3.5a

Common Notions About Women and Work

Common Notions About Women	*Non-Teaching Staff (%)*			*Teaching Staff (%)*		
	Female	*Male*	*All*	*Female*	*Male*	*All*
Notions about females carried from home to workplace	46.8	43.1	45.0	56.1	51.8	53.5
Women should not lose sight of their gender status when dealing with men	46.8	47.1	47.0	35.6	43.4	40.5
Gender position of women determines workplace relations	45.6	47.5	46.6	56.2	54.6	54.8
Sex is more important in recruiting women than qualification	17.3	28.0	22.5	5.5	13.3	10.6
Gender roles and stereotypes are more important in job recruitment and assignments	19.0	22.2	20.6	8.2	11.2	10.6
Workplace job assignments are influenced by gender roles of women and men	27.0	30.2	28.6	34.3	30.8	31.8
Females better at certain tasks than males	59.1	48.0	53.6	61.7	58.1	59.5
Females should be assigned certain workplace tasks and not others	23.2	28.9	26.0	17.8	23.1	21.2
Females only fit for certain positions in university	11.4	18.7	14.9	2.7	4.2	3.7
Females not fit to head; easily manipulated by men	8.0	16.0	11.9	5.5	6.3	6.0

Source: Field Date: 2001.

TABLE 3.5b

Common Notions about Females

Notions	Students		Non-Teaching staff		Teaching staff		All	
	Count	*Per cent*	*Count*	*Per cent*	*Count*	*Per cent*	*Count*	*Per cent*
Girls of some ethnic/religious group are likely to be sexual harassment victims	180	12.6	44	9.5	21	9.7	245	11.6
Presentation of women in some cultures makes them likely victims	766	53.8	217	47.0	101	46.5	1084	51.5

Source: Field Data 2001.

females should be restricted to certain types of jobs (Table 3.5a). Such assumptions about women are important in the sense that they help to determine how gendered the university is in terms of work relations and in effect show how supportive people will be of women who suffer any work-related gender discrimination or are perceived as having transgressed known gender norms.

Table 3.5b covers general notions about women and therefore includes responses from students as well. Here, few staff respondents (about 12 per cent), agreed that one's ethnic background alone is enough attraction for sexual harassment. On the other hand, about half of all respondents agreed that it is the way women are presented in some cultures that can make them victims of sexual harassment. What is being examined here is whether stereotypes feed into people's attitudes and make it easier for them to treat some people in a certain way as a result of the common notions held about people of a certain background.

The predominant view amongst respondents on the university campuses is that the sexual nature of an act is what should designate it as sexual harassment. Such a view leaves out forms of hostile environment sexually-harassing experiences which in most instances are directed at females. Thus, even though the females at the receiving end will feel traumatized they will have very little room for redress if the definition of sexual harassment is not expanded to cover gender-based harassment.

The perceptions of respondents reveal an admission that the experience of harassment is not the same for males as for females. When males get harassed, they feel provoked to harass the females they perceive as their harassers, harassing experience for females does not present the same opportunity. For the male, the experience results in harassing someone in return. For the female, the question of retaliating does not arise. Rather, the harassing experience demeans her to such an extent that divulging any information on the harassment she has suffered will lead to a loss of status and dignity. The emotional impact in both instances will vary if for males the experience results in redeeming a lost image through the opportunity to react. Females are not presented with similar opportunities to redeem their sense of violation or lost dignity.

It is clear from the perceptions that ideas about what is sexually-appropriate female behaviour get centre stage in the way people perceive sexual harassment on the university campuses in Ghana. The perceptions of respondents and workshop participants justify some forms of sexual harassment, pardon male harassers and make females responsible for being harassed. These assumptions also highlight sex as a central feature of any female and male encounters. The concern here is the extent to which such assumptions can severely limit support networks for female professional and academic advancement.

The differences in female and male concepts of sex bring out two issues. One is the woman's dignity and her ability to regulate her sexual behaviour at her own dictate. The other is the man's ego conceived in this particular context as sexual prowess and which spells out appropriate male response to a provocative female behaviour. Clearly, female and male notion of sex is bound to clash around the definition of sexual harassment and what behaviours should be labelled as sexually-harassing and sanctioned. When such a situation arises in an environment dominated by perceptions that place women's sexuality at the disposal of men then females will have little control over their sexuality and as a result little protection from the sexual harassment policy. Respondents' perceptions, therefore, highlight the power relations between the sexes: the vulnerability of females and how this operates to inform attitudes that feed into sexual harassment. The starting point of the policy will have to be education on gender relations, patriarchy and sexuality.

Chapter 4

THE EXPERIENCE OF SEXUAL HARASSMENT ON THE UNIVERSITY CAMPUSES

Introduction

The previous chapter discussed the perceptions of various members of the university communities and tried to highlight the policy implications of such perceptions. This chapter discusses the actual experience of sexual harassment as reported by the respondents. The prevalence of sexual harassment on the university campuses, according to the respondents, was much higher than was reported. Respondents believed that most people experiencing sexual harassment were reluctant to report for fear of stigmatization. The workshops revealed incidents of sexual harassment that had not been captured in the field work. Presenters at the dissemination workshops noted reports of lecturers who use their positions to coerce student into unwanted sexual relationships and the operation of a gang of rapists who drugged their female dates in order to have sex with them.

Field work revealed a few cases of sexual harassment that had been investigated on the university campuses. The research team found documentation on three such cases on three different campuses. All cases involved students accusing lecturers for having sexually-harassed them. In two instances, the students were unable to substantiate their complaints. At UEW, the female student who was unable to substantiate her case was punished to lose one semester. The sanction was withdrawn upon an order from the high court. At UCC, the lecturer decided to pursue a civil case of defamation in the law court after the students had failed to substantiate their case before a committee set up by the Vice-chancellor. The court found the students guilty of defamation and the lecturer awarded damages. The ruling on this case came long after the students had completed their course of study at UCC. The third instance was at the UG; the lecturer in question was found guilty of having physically assaulted a male student in what was presented by the student as rivalry over a female student friend. The result was a code of ethics designed to regulate relations between lecturers and students. In each of the three cases, a special committee was set up by the Vice-chancellor or principal. The two cases at UEW and UCC raise questions about the legal status of a university policy on sexual harassment within the contest of state law.

Types of Sexual Harassment Experiences on University Campuses

Several forms of sexual harassment experiences were reported by respondents on the various campuses. The experience of sexual harassment was not limited to one category of persons. However the proportion of female respondents who had suffered sexual harassment was slightly higher (60 per cent female as against 50 per cent of the males). Sixty four per cent (64 per cent) of students on the whole, 29 per cent of teaching staff and 26 per cent of non-teaching staff had experienced sexual harassment (Table 4.1). The proportion of female students who reported having experienced sexual harassment was highest (about 67 per cent, Table 4.1). This confirms Wamahiu and Chege's (1996) assertion that women tend to suffer more sexual harassment than men and the perceptions of respondents that female students are the most vulnerable to sexual harassment.

The specific forms of sexual harassment that respondents had experienced fell within the three groups of harassing behaviours discussed in earlier chapters. The forms of experiences were not exclusive to a particular sex. However, females' experiences of sexual harassment were mainly those that made them feel uncomfortable, threatened, demeaned or violated their rights (Table 4.2). Male experiences were on the other hand, expressed as those that aroused them sexually.

The experiences reported conformed to those behaviours that had been identified earlier by respondents and workshop participants as sexual harassment (*see* Chapter 3). There were experiences that subjected the victim to a hostile environment, sexual coercion, and others that were sexually-provocative. The specific forms of sexual harassment experienced on the campuses that tended to create a hostile environment were:

TABLE 4.1

Proportion of Respondents Who Have Experienced Sexual Harassment

Response	Students (%)			Teaching Staff (%)			Non-Teaching Staff (%)			All Respondents (%)		
	Female	Male	All	Female	Male	All	Female	Male	All	Female	Male	All
Experienced	66.8	60.9	64.0	37.2	24.7	28.6	33.3	20.0	26.4	60.2	49.5	54.7
No Experience	33.2	39.1	36.0	62.8	75.3	71.4	66.7	80.0	73.6	39.8	50.5	45.3
Total	100.0	100.0	100.0	100.0	100.0	100.0	100.0	100.0	100.0	100.0	100.0	100.0

Source: Field data, 2001.

TABLE 4.2

Types of Sexual Harassment Experienced on the Campuses

Sexual harassment Experienced	Students (%)		Teaching staff (%)		Non-Teaching staff (%)		All Respondents (%)	
	Female	Male	Female	Male	Female	Male	Female	Male
Unwanted physical contact	63.3	33.1	56.3	8.3	46.2	18.8	61.7	30.3
Mode of dressing	5.4	19.1	0	25.0	7.7	43.8	5.3	20.9
Unwanted exposure of sexually sensitive parts	5.1	16.7	6.3	25.0	15.4	12.5	5.9	17.2
Unwanted compliment/Remarks	6.3	5.1	25.0	16.7	15.4	0	7.8	5.7
Rape/Forced Sex	6.3	6.3	0	0	0	0	5.6	8.1
Exposure to pornographic material	6.3	5.4	6.3	4.2	0	6.3	5.9	5.4
Sitting posture	1.9	5.4	0	12.5	3.8	6.3	2.0	6.1
Others*	5.4	5.8	6.3	8.3	11.5	12.5	5.9	6.4
TOTAL	100.0 (315)	100.0 (257)	100.0 (16)	100.0 (24)	100.0 (26)	100.0 (16)	100.0 (358)	100.0 (297)

*Includes, looks & vocal intimidation.
Source: Field Data: 2001.

1. Physical harassment in the form of unwanted physical contacts (unwanted fondling, kissing, grabbing, touching and rubbing);
2. Verbal harassment in the form of:
    i. Unwanted remarks/compliments (teasing of a sexual nature, sexual jokes, telephone sex);
    ii. Vocal intimidation (jeering, booing, name calling, cat calls, whistling and hissing);
3. Graphic harassment in the form of exposure to pornographic material;
4. Gestural harassment in the form of winking.

The most prevalent type of sexual harassment reported was unwanted physical contact, which includes unwanted fondling, kissing, grabbing, touching and rubbing. Forty eight per cent of respondents who reported having ever suffered sexual harassment had been subjected to some form of unwanted physical contact. Females experienced this more than males and it was the form of sexual harassment frequently meted out on females by males (61 per cent females as against 30 per cent males see Table 4.2). It was the form of sexual harassment experienced by the largest proportion of all categories of females and male students (63 per cent of female students, 56 per cent of female teaching staff, 46 per cent of female non-teaching staff and 33 per cent of male students). Students had suffered mostly this form of sexual harassment followed by teaching staff and non-teaching staff.

Unwanted compliment was experienced by 7 per cent of the respondents. This consisted of 6 per cent of the female student victims, 5 per cent of male student victims, 25 per cent of female teaching staff victims, and 17 per cent male teaching staff victims, 15 per cent of non-teaching female staff victims. On the whole, the proportion of females who reported that they had suffered this type of harassment was higher (8 per cent) than that of the males (6 per cent) (Table 4.2). Workshop participants reported incidents of lectures who use their lectures as occasions to verbally assult female students who are resisting their sexual advances. Respondents who had experienced exposure to pornographic materials were mainly students, 6 per cent of female students and 5.4 per cent of male students (Table 4.2).

The second group of experiences reported covered those behaviours that were sexually-coercive, forced sex or rape. Only students reported the experience of rape or forced sex. There were an equal proportion of female to male students (6 per cent each) who had experienced rape/forced sex (Table 4.2).

The third group of sexually-harassing experiences reported were those that respondents claimed aroused them sexually (sexual provocation). Sexually-provocative experiences reported were of three types those that were geared towards soliciting sex, sexually-offensive behaviour and experiences that aroused male sexual urge. They took the form of:

1. Mode of dressing;
2. Exposure of unwanted sexually sensitive parts;
3. Improper sitting posture.

The first type was derived from what has been described earlier as sexual corruption (Pereira, 2002). This referred to situations where females peddle sexual favours for money or material goods, or other benefits like job promotion or grades. The group discussion sessions and the dissemination workshops, for example, revealed a phenomenon described as "sexually-transmitted grades". Female students were reported to be trading sex for opportunities to better their academic standing either to have their grades enhanced ("sexually-transmitted grades") or to see examination questions. Male teaching assistants and lecturers were identified as being at the receiving end of such favours.

The prevalent fashion at the time of the study was made up of tight fitting clothes that hug the body and sometimes expose female breasts and abdomen. The general attitude on the campuses was that this form of dressing was provocative and the main cause of increasing levels of sexual harassment in the country in general and on the university campuses to be particular. The extent of these concerns came to a head when in 2001, on the university of Ghana campus, a section of the female students went on demonstration against the "indecent dressing" of some of their female colleagues. These concerns notwithstanding, most female students almost in some apparent disregard for such concerns continue to dress this way in conformity with the predominant fashion of the day.

Mode of dressing ranked second after unwanted physical contact as the form of sexual harassment that respondents reported to have experienced. Almost 12 per cent of the 655 respondents who reported having experienced sexual harassment mentioned mode of dressing as the form the harassment they suffered took. Mode of dressing was found to be one of the most prevalent types of sexual harassment that males reported having suffered. In all, 21 per cent males as against 5 per cent females had experienced this type of harassment. Nineteen per cent (19 per cent) male students, 25 per cent male teaching staff and 44 per cent male non-teaching staff indicated that they had suffered from this type of harassment (Table 4.2).

Another form of sexual provocation was unwanted exposure of sexually sensitive parts which was experienced mostly by male teaching staff (25 per cent), 17 per cent male students and 15 per cent female non-teaching staff (Table 4.2). Seventeen per cent of the male and 6 per cent of the female respondents who had ever been sexually-harassed had experienced this form of harassment (Table 4.2). Sitting posture, another form of sexual harassment reported, was experienced by 4 per cent of the 655 respondents, mostly males (6 per cent males as against 2 per cent females). About 13 per cent of male teaching staff, 5 per cent of male students and 2 per cent of the female students reported this experience (Table 4.2).

Sources and Location of Sexual Harassment Experiences

It is equally important to identify the persons most likely to harass others just as it is to identify those most vulnerable to sexual harassment. The source of harassment is crucial in that it can determine how far power relations at play in the experience can constrain reaction and the extent to which the harassed will seek some institutional protection from the experience.

An analysis of responses from respondents who had experienced unwanted physical contact identified male students as being the most likely to harass others in this manner. Between 86 and 100 per cent of the three categories of female respondents mentioned males as their harassers. Whereas 54 per cent of female student respondents mentioned male students as their harassers, 11 per cent mentioned lecturers and another 6 per cent mentioned senior staff. Female teaching staff respondents, on the other hand, were more likely to be harassed by male students; 33 per cent reported that their harassers had been male students. Non-teaching staff were more likely to be harassed by male lecturers

(33 per cent) and male students (25 per cent). In most instances, harassers were of the opposite sex. Same sex harassment, however, was experienced more by male students in the form of forced sex. Male students named males as their harassers. Harassment which took the form of sexual provocation was reported to have been inflicted more by females on males. Female students were identified as most likely to harass staff this way.

Sexual harassment was experienced in every possible place on the university campuses. As it is to be expected, respondents' experiences occurred in the locations where they carried out most of their activities. Female students, however, were more likely to suffer sexual harassment in a wider variety of locations like their rooms or halls of residence, the lecture theatres, on the streets and in the offices on the university campus. Lecturers, on the other hand, suffered more cases of sexual harassment in the offices and the lecture theatres. Non-teaching staff had their experiences limited mainly to the offices. Forced sex or rape occurred more in student rooms and offices on the university campuses.

It appears that the experience of sexual harassment on the university campuses is gendered in its source and the form that it takes with differences in female and male forms of sexual harassment. Over three quarters of all female respondents who had ever suffered sexual harassment had gone through some experience that created a hostile environment as against 43 per cent of the males. The majority of respondents who had experience of sexual harassment in the form of sexual provocation were males (44 per cent as against 13 per cent for females).

Likely Causes of Sexual Harassment

Respondents were asked to explain what factors in their estimation might have been the likely cause of their sexual harassment experiences. Their responses have been grouped into two: those related to the victims and those related to the harassers.

Those related to the victims included factors that played up their vulnerability like:

1. Need for financial assistance;
2. Fear of poor academic performance;

3. Lobbying for votes;
4. Newly-recruited staff.

The second group of likely causes that respondents identified that were attributed to their harassers have been grouped into those that derive from the power of the perpetrators, and place them in a position to take advantage of the victim, like granting students academic favours. Other likely causes that derived from the perpetrators were related to issues of sex and sexuality like:

1. Satisfaction of sexual urge and lack of self-discipline;
2. Expression of love;
3. Search for partner;
4. Drunkenness and desire for sex.

Responses from the victims indicated that the greatest cause of sexual harassment by both male and female perpetrators was attractiveness of victim. Whereas the second main cause of sexual harassment by male perpetrators was satisfaction of sexual urge and lack of self-discipline by the male harassers (28.5 per cent), the second main cause of sexual harassment by female perpetrators was expression of love by the female perpetrators (26 per cent) (Table 4.3).

Respondents also reported that certain behaviours of theirs had been interpreted by their harassers as invitation to have sex. Some of these were:

1. Over socialization;
2. Friendliness;
3. Kindness and being nice to people;
4. Being out-spoken;
5. Mode of dressing;
6. Physical contact.

Table 4.4 shows behaviours that respondents who had been victims of sexual harassment believed their harassers had interpreted as invitation to harass them sexually. Friendliness/kindness and being nice to people ranked highest. It was reported by 34.4 per cent of the respondents followed by mode of dressing (23.8 per cent), over-socialization (23.1

TABLE 4.3

Perception of Respondents about the Likely Causes of Their Sexual Harassment Experiences

Causes of Harassment	Students (%)		Teaching staff (%)		Non-teaching (%)		All respondents (%)		
	Female	Male	Female	Male	Female	Male	Female	Male	All
Attractiveness of victim	39.3	34.4	27.3	14.3	50.0	62.5	39.2	35.1	37.0
Satisfaction of sexual urge/lack of self-discipline by harasser	17.9	31.1	18.2	21.4	0	12.5	17.1	28.5	23.1
Expression of love by harasser	28.6	17.0	0	14.3	0	6.3	25.8	16.5	20.9
Search for a partner by harasser	7.1	2.4	9.1	7.1	0	0	6.9	2.9	4.8
Victim's need for financial assistance	2.0	4.2	18.2	7.1	0	0	2.8	4.1	3.5
Victim's fear of poor academic performance	4.1	3.3	0	0	0	0	3.7	2.9	3.3
Others	1.0	7.5	27.3	35.7	50.0	18.8	4.6	9.9	7.4
TOTAL	100.0 (196)	100.0 (212)	100.0 (11)	100.0 (14)	100.0 (10)	100.0 (16)	100.0 (217)	100.0 (242)	100.0 (459)

Source: Field data, 2001.

per cent) and out-spoken nature (6.8 per cent). Responses from students and teaching staff followed the same order as the general one; however, that of the non-teaching staff was different (Table 4.4). To the non-teaching staff, mode of dressing was not a major behaviour interpreted as invitation for harassment; it was rather over socialization. There was not much difference between the responses of the sexes.

Reaction to Sexual Harassment

The reactions of respondents who had fallen victim to the various types of sexual harassment were varied. They included those reactions which instantly sent clear messages that the action or behaviour was unwanted like:

1. Putting up strong resistance;
2. Giving warnings;
3. Rejection;
4. Screaming and shouting for help;
5. Demanding explanation from the perpetrator.

Some respondents reacted silently to their sexually-harassing experiences. They put up behaviours that showed that they were not in favour of the experience they were being subjected to by:

1. Putting up no reaction at all;
2. Ignoring the perpetrator and his/her behaviour;
3. Withdrawing from the perpetrator;
4. Moving away from the scene or;
5. Closing their eyes.

Others were unable to ward off the reaction. Some were induced to have sex with their harassers or honoured the invitations of their harassers or smiled back.

The common reactions that were given by the student victims were the type that showed that the behaviours were unwanted. They were a mixture of the vocal and non-vocal reactions. Most of the student victims of sexual harassment (106 out of 527) reacted by putting up strong resistance especially to unwanted physical contact, and rape. The second most common reaction by students was ignoring the perpetrator and the

TABLE 4.4

Behaviour of Respondents Interpreted as Invitation to Harass

Behaviour/Nature	Students (%)		Teaching staff (%)		Non-teaching (%)		All respondents (%)		
	Female	Male	Female	Male	Female	Male	Female	Male	All
Friendliness/kindness/nice to people	34.1	34.2	45.5	28.6	25.0	36.4	34.6	34.2	34.4
Mode of dressing	24.9	23.7	27.3	28.6	0.0	9.1	24.5	23.2	23.8
Over-socialization	23.7	23.7	18.2	0.0	50.0	9.1	23.9	22.4	23.1
Being outspoken	5.8	6.8	0.0	14.3	0.0	27.3	5.3	8.0	6.8
Sexually-attractive, beautiful	4.6	5.9	9.1	14.3	0.0	9.1	4.8	6.3	5.6
Physical contact	6.4	4.6	0.0	14.3	0.0	9.1	5.9	5.1	5.4
Others	0.6	1.0	0.0	0.0	25.0	0.0	1.1	0.8	0.9
TOTAL	100.0 (173)	100.0 (219)	100.0 (4)	100.0 (11)	100.0 (4)	100.0 (11)	100.0 (188)	100.0 (237)	100.0 (425)

Source: Field data, 2001

behaviour (92 out of 527). This was the reaction to experiences like "mode of dressing" (16 out of 54), "unwanted exposure of sexually sensitive parts" (13 out of 56) "unwanted compliment" and "sitting posture" (8 out of 31 and 3 out of 17 respectively).

Staff respondents' (teaching and non teaching) reaction to sexual harassment were also verbal and non-verbal. Unlike the reaction put up by students, they all showed that the behaviours or actions were unwanted. Out of 75 staff respondents who reacted to sexual harassment, 23 ignored the act, 13 put up strong resistance and 10 rejected the advances. Seven gave warnings to the perpetrators and another 7 demanded explanation from the harassers. The most common reaction put up against unwanted exposure of sexually-sensitive parts, mode of dressing and telephone sex was to ignore them. Regarding unwanted physical contact and unwanted compliment the most common reaction was putting up strong resistance. Student and staff respondents will put up strong resistance to unwanted physical contact but will simply ignore "provocative" dressing and unwanted compliment. The third category of reaction, that did not show that the advances were unwanted, was put up by students only.

Workshop reports noted that the decision on the part of victims to remain silent and not show any strong objection to their sexually harassing experiencies was dictated by circumstances such as fear of victimization and stigmatization as well as difficulty in substantiating that the events actually occurred. Some non-teaching staff victims of sexual harassment opted for departmental transfers to escape their harassers. Generally, one's response cannot be taken as a good index of whether or not an event is wanted. Power relations and the isolation of the victim can constrain reaction. In some instances, the power of conformity is very strong and females sometimes put up with sexual harassment in male-dominated circles in order to get accepted. Thus, the environment in which the experience takes place can inhibit objections to sexually-harassing situations. Bortei-Doku Aryeetey (2004) attributes women failure to act promptly to avert sexually harassing experiences to sheer confusion, or fear, deference, friendship and other emotive or relational factors that get in the way of good reason or common sense. Socialization that preaches submissiveness among women hardly prepares them to be assertive in order to be able to discourage people who try to take advantage of them *(ibid.)*.

Effect of Sexual Harassment

About 76 per cent of the respondents who have had experience of sexual harassment indicated that the experience had affected them in one way or the other. Two hundred and eighty one (281) were females and two hundred and sixteen (216) were males. With the exception of female teaching staff, the most common type of effect sexual harassment had on the victims was emotional disturbances and depression (40 per cent) (see Table 4.5). This was followed by the different types of behavioural change towards the opposite sex, one of which was distrust for the opposite sex (20.5 per cent). The most common effect that sexual harassment had on female teaching staff was distrust for the opposite sex followed by emotional disturbances and other behavioural changes towards the opposite sex. Some respondents who had been victims of sexual harassment reported that they became extremely careful about the opposite sex (13 per cent). Some (11 per cent) developed hatred for the opposite sex and others (7 per cent) withdrew from the opposite sex. Other student victims failed their examinations. Others reported effects on their reproductive system such as infertility, pregnancy and frequent erection.

TABLE 4.5

Effect of Sexual Harassment on Victim

Effect	Female (%)	Male (%)	All (%)
Emotionally disturbed/depressed	40.6	38.9	39.8
Distrust for the opposite sex	22.8	17.6	20.5
Extremely careful about the opposite sex	11.4	14.4	12.7
Hatred for the opposite sex	14.2	6.9	11.1
Withdrawal from the opposite sex	5.3	8.8	6.8
Educated on the subject/learnt a lesson	2.1	6.0	3.8
Interest in sex/sexual relationship aroused	1.1	4.6	2.6
Others	2.5	2.8	2.6
TOTAL	100.0	100.0	100.0
	(281)	(216)	(497)

Source: Field data, 2001.

Certain types of sexual harassment carry with them some stigma and, as a result, friends and relations did not want to be associated with the victims. Friends and relations withdrew from the victims. There were even changes in relationships with the victims in some cases. Others withdrew from the victims for fear that they might have the same harassment meted on them.

Sexual harassment did not affect only the victims; those around the victims also suffered from the harassment. People had disrespect for the opposite sex because of the impact of the sexual harassment their colleagues or friends had suffered. Others pledged to support the fight against sexual harassment.

Workshop presentations revealed wider-ranging impact of sexual harassment in the form of breakdown in workplace discipline. Some junior staff in some universities were reported to have escaped the control of their superiors and were flouting orders with arrogance and pride[17]. Other members of staff become apathetic, paralyzed by the fear of intimidation by senior colleagues. Collegial work relation suffered a breakdown because they were marred by rumours, rivalry and suspicion.

The effects of sexual harassment were diverse and of different degrees. Some were damaging and permanent. Most of the effects were psychological and victims may carry these for the rest of their lives. Emotional disturbance, the most common effect, can affect the academic work or job of the victims. The changes in behaviour towards the opposite sex can affect the victims' relationships with the opposite sex and even marriage. The types of effect of sexual harassment on the sexes were almost the same. About 80 per cent of the females and 71 per cent of males who had experienced sexual harassment indicated that it has had effect on them.

Conclusion

The experience of sexual harassment on the university campuses had three major features: the forms the harassing experience took, the most recurrent reaction to harassment and the nature of its impact. Generally, the experience of sexual harassment was gendered with females reporting that their experience took the form of hostile environment sexual harassment and males, sexual provocation. Questions of sexuality are raised here because the interpretation of female behaviour as sexually provocative brings out what is sexually acceptable and the extent to which the determination of what is culturally acceptable gives women room to express their sexuality on their own terms. Trading sexuality for favours generates an academic environment which undermines female desire and potential to excel academically.

The experience of sexual harassment is not without resistance. The study found that even though some respondents resisted, there were others who failed to resist. As noted earlier, failure to resist cannot be interpreted that the behaviour was wanted. The context of the experience and its source can constrain reaction. That the experience has been recorded as sexually harassing should suffice as an indication that it was unwanted. Managing sexual harassment should pose a great challenge to the universities. The next chapter explores how the universities are faring in this direction and what exists that can form the basis for a policy that affirms equal rights of all members.

Chapter 5

SEXUAL HARASSMENT MANAGEMENT SYSTEMS IN THE UNIVERSITIES

Introduction

Sexual harassment was treated as one of the several possible breaches of rules and regulations within the universities. UEW was the only university that had evolved a sexual harassment policy at the time of the study. The provisions of the policy which were binding on all members of the university community were only available in the students' handbook. At UG, a code of conduct, evolved in response to a proven case of assault meted out by a lecturer to a student, outlined measures for regulating student lecturer relationship. This code of conduct was limited to relationships between senior members and students, prescribed behaviour considered appropriate or otherwise and proposed sanctions for misdemeanour. Some universities had sections in the student's handbook that identified some forms of sexual harassment as offences that could attract sanctions.

This chapter explores the system or structures used on the various campuses to manage sexual harassment. The discussion covers respondents' knowledge and attitudes towards the system available for managing sexual harassment. It covers also the level of utilization of these structures by the various categories of respondents and the outcome of discussions at the dissemination workshops.

Knowledge about Sexual Harassment Regulatory System

Non-teaching and student respondents generally were not aware of the specific rules or regulations on sexual harassment operating in their universities. About one in three key person respondents were certain that there were no formal rules and regulations on sexual harassment. Over half of the teaching staff respondents admitted that they had no knowledge of such a system or that they believed that none existed on the campus. A few attempted a guess and supplied a list of possible sanctions such as dismissals, bonding, counselling, suspension; others mentioned the rule prohibiting males from visiting female halls of residence after a certain hour in the day as a sexual harassment regulation. The students' handbook was mentioned by most respondents as a possible source of rules on sexual harassment. Some students also mentioned that they were cautioned against sexual harassment during the orientation programmes organized for them in their first week as students in the university.

About 40 per cent student respondents attempted to guess which departments or sections on their campuses handled sexual harassment cases. The list yielded responses like all departments, Dean of Students, University administration, Hall Counsellors, the Counselling Centre the SRC and the Department of Psychology. Most of the respondents mentioned the Office of the Dean of Students as the section on campus responsible for handling sexual harassment cases.

The inaccuracies in terms of the responses supplied suggested not so much the ignorance on the part of respondents but rather the fact that there was no clear-cut system on any of the campuses for handling sexual harassment. Sexual harassment was perceived by the universities as one of the many problems of discipline that might beset any institution of its kind. The general system for handling all disciplinary cases should suffice to deal with sexual harassment. Thus, cases involving students whether as harassers or harassed were more likely to be referred to the offices of the Deans of Students. For staff, both teaching and non-teaching the Deans of Faculties were the most likely officers required to handle such cases. The various structures that handled sexual harassment cases were, therefore, determined to a large extent by the people involved.

Departments/Sections Ever Used to Handle Sexual Harassment

None of the public universities studied had an office set up to handle sexual harassment cases. No guidelines existed for determining the facility that someone facing a sexually-harassing experience could use. Sexual harassment was treated as one of the many disciplinary or social problems that members of the university community face. Depending on the nature of the problem or its impact, persons facing any sexually-harassing experiences could decide to speak to any office of their choice.

Students, for example, might confide in their hall counsellors or if the experience is physically threatening they might go to the Office of the Dean of Students or Students' Affairs. Some Deans of Students will handle only certain cases of sexual harassment and refer those they considered outside their jurisdiction to the counselling centre, for example. Those who act do so by giving advice after a careful analysis of the reports made. Non-teaching staff will use the central university administration or the Registrar's office and teaching staff their heads of department or deans. When sexual harassment cases are received, the personnel responsible refer most of the complainants to another office like the Counselling Centre or the disciplinary committee. Heads of departments refer the case to the Deans of Faculties or Schools.

About two out of every five key person respondents belonged to departments which had dealt with some sexual harassment case. Out of this number, about 45 per cent belonged to sections that normally had the responsibility for handling sexual harassment cases. On the whole, few respondents had used some university facility to handle sexual harassment cases (2.4 per cent). The proportion of key person respondents who reported having used some university department or section to handle sexual harassment cases was higher (20 per cent). Out of the 71 key person respondents, 15 reported ever using some section or department to handle sexual harassment cases. Of this number, seven used the counselling centre, two used Hall Counsellors, another two used a special committee and one each used the Disciplinary Committee, Welfare Office and the Students' Affairs Office. Key persons acknowledge the procedures and structures for dealing with sexual harassment were inadequate and thus constrain both managers and victims of sexual harassment in terms of options for seeking redress.

Table 5.1 gives a breakdown of departments and sections within the universities that respondents have ever used to seek redress for their sexual harassment experiences. A small proportion of students (about 1 per cent) have used some section or department within the university to handle a sexual harassment case. More teaching than non-teaching staff have also used some university facility to handle sexual harassment cases. It appears that respondents are more ready to use a facility for redress on behalf of others than on their own behalf. Sections and departments used by individual respondents do not differ from those used by key person respondents. They include the Counselling Centre, used by most respondents, suggesting that sexual harassment is seen as a behavioural trait that requires counselling and not sanctioning. The next is the Hall Counsellors who appear the most obvious choice of students who will be seeking advice and counselling about how to handle sexually-harassing experience and not to get their harasser sanctioned. Non-teaching staff respondents, on the other hand, prefer the Central Administration. Very few use the Office of the Dean of Students. It is not easy interpreting the preference for non-sanctioning sections owing to the low levels of responses to this particular question. One issue that is certain though is the fact that very few people are using some university facility to handle a sexually-harassing experience (Table 5.1).

TABLE 5.1

Departments/Sections Ever Used to Manage Sexual Harassment Cases

Sections or department ever used	Students		Non-Teaching staff		Teaching staff		Key persons		All	
	No.	%	No.	%	No.	%	No.	%	No.	%
Counselling centre	4	0.3	3	0.6	3	1.4	7	10.4	17	0.8
Hall counsellors	4	0.3	–	–	2	0.9	2	3.0	8	0.38
University administration/ Registrars' office	–	–	6	1.3	2	1	–	–	8	0.4
Disciplinary/Special committee	1	0.1	2	0.4	1	0.5	3	4.5	7	0.3
Dean of students	1	0.1	1	0.2	–	–	1	1.5	3	0.1
Heads of department	–	–	2	0.4	–	–	–	–	2	0.1
The SRC	1	0.1	1	0.2	1	0.5	–	–	3	0.1
Chaplain/Welfare office	–	–	1	0.2			1	1.5	2	0.1
TOTAL	11	0.9	16	3.3	9	4.3	14	20.9	50	2.4

Source: Field study 2001

According to respondents, the number of sexual harassment cases reported was too few to warrant the setting up of special structures to deal with sexual harassment cases. Several reasons advanced to explain why such few cases of sexual harassment get reported pointed to low levels of confidence in the present structures. For one thing, the bureaucratic process for seeking redress is long and delays justice. For another, the justice system treats sexual harassment as a civil case or one that requires emotional counselling. Such factors undermine the readiness with which persons suffering sexual harassment would want to pursue justice. Peer influence can encourage as it can discourage victims from reporting experience suffered. There were reported cases of friends discouraging harassed colleagues from reporting their experience because of the fear of attracting the scorn of the community. The perception was that people who suffer harassment are stigmatized and the fear of being stigmatized prevents people who have experienced harassment from seeking redress. Some do not have confidence in the ability of the system to protect them from powerful harassers. It was a general belief that students who report lecturers who sexually harass them stand the risk of being punished by these lecturers. Similar assertions were made by Bortei-Doku Aryeetey (2004) when she stated that many sufferers of sexual harassment were aware that the backlash from seeking redress invariably affected them more than their harassers, they risked being transferred, fired, demoted or marginalized. The workshops noted that fear of retaliatory actions from powerful harassers constrains students and junior staff members from reporting. Some victims are unsure of their rights. Male harassers often trivialize their actions and claim in some instances that sexually-harassing behaviour on their part was meant to create fun.

The low levels of reporting, therefore, was more of a reflection of the confidence which people have in the system in place for handling sexual harassment and not of the levels of incidence. Victims might very well be waiting for an efficient system that provides some protection to report. The returns for reporting, it is believed, must be worthwhile. The absence of clear and efficient policy is believed to be a disincentive. This means that no system for managing sexual harassment will ever be set up if it has to await a sustained high frequency of reporting the occurrence of the phenomenon.

Levels of satisfaction gained from using a facility form the basis for developing confidence and shows the extent to which respondents are likely to use such a facility again and then recommend it to others with similar experience. Students appeared to derive more satisfaction from the facilities they utilize than non-teaching staff respondents (see Table 5.2). It appears that a greater proportion of all individual respondents who have ever used the Counselling Centre to deal with sexual harassment cases were satisfied with the outcome (70 per cent). No respondents reported getting satisfaction from using Hall Counsellors.

TABLE 5.2

Respondents Expressing Satisfaction with Facility Ever Used

Sections or department ever used	Students		Non-Teaching staff		Teaching staff		All	
	No.	%	No.	%	No.	%	No.	%
Counselling centre/psychology department	4	100	1	33.3	2	66.7	7	70
Dean of students	1	25	0	0.0	1	50.0	2	33.3
Disciplinary committee	0	0	1	16.7	0	0.0	1	12.5
University administration/ Registrars	1	100	1	50.0	0	0.0	2	50
Heads of department	1	100	1	100.0	0	0.0	2	100
The SRC	0	0	1	50.0	0	0.0	1	50
Chaplain/Welfare office	1	100	0	0.0	0	0.0	1	33.3
Hall counsellors	0	0	0	0.0	0	0.0	0	0
TOTAL	8	72.7	5	31.3	3	33.3	16	44.4

Source: Field study 2001.

The Entry Points for Developing University Sexual Harassment Policies

Important entry points like the strategic plans or statutes of the universities were acknowledged as useful basis for incorporating sexual harassment policies. The statutes and strategic plans are overarching policy documents from which sector specific policies emanate. These two sources set the framework for the recognition of rights and aspects of university life that should be covered by specific documents. At the time of the study, some universities were at various stages of evolving their strategic plans. The UDS and UEW, for example, were in the process of mainstreaming gender concerns into their strategic plans. These documents were unavailable for study but some workshop presentations noted that sexual harassment was seen as an important component of gender relations within the universities[18].

University of Cape Coast launched its strategic plan in June 2003. The mission statement of the plan affirms the position of the UCC as an equal opportunity university. The document is, however, silent on specific efforts to create an environment supportive of women and generally on issues of gender discrimination. None of its ten strategic thrusts mention even remotely, sexual harassment. The key thrust 7 which aims at creating "an organizational culture that enhances efficiency, discipline and commitment" provides one of the areas where sexual harassment could have been incorporated. The key thrust 10 which comes closest to raising gender concerns is aimed primarily at promoting the image of the university "as one which encourages an equal number of male and female admissions" (University of Cape Coast Corporate Strategy 2003). The 2003 strategic plan of UCC provides several openings for incorporating sexual harassment policy on the university campus irrespective of its gender neutral onendation.

As noted earlier, UEW has developed a sexual harassment policy which was already in force and applied to all staff and students as well as all who transact business with the university. The UEW sexual harassment policy is based on the concern that sexual harassment is discriminatory and harmful to the general well-being and dignity of individuals. The policy is also concerned about the fact that sexual harassment stifles the healthy environment required for the promotion and realization of the objectives of the university because it affects the performance of both staff and students.

The UEW sexual harassment policy is aimed at raising the level of awareness of its community about the illegality of sexual harassment in Ghana and to encourage a change in the negative attitudes towards females and finally establish a woman-friendly atmosphere on its campuses. The policy is, therefore, based on the principles that affirms the illegality of sexual harassment in every form at UEW and as well as the rights of all members. The basic principles, for example, state that sexual harassment in every form is prohibited and constitutes a punishable offence; sexual harassment is a violation of the basic human rights and the right to academic freedom and freedom of expression. Other principles that guide the policy insist that all members of the UEW community should have access to all its facilities and services without fear of sexual harassment. In addition, persons in positions of responsibility should not use their position as tools for demanding favours or coercing others into unwanted situations.

The policy mentions the establishment of desks on the three campuses of UEW at Winneba, Kumasi and Asante Mampong. These desks are supposed to have officers and a team of advisors. The policy outlines two main procedures for handling cases of sexual harassment: formal and informal. The informal procedure consists of verbal complaint on sexual harassment lodged with the desk officer or any of the advisors. Any of the two officers is required to mediate for an amicable settlement of the complaint. The harasser may be asked to render a written or verbal apology with a promise not to repeat the offensive act. The formal action is taken when an informal complaint is made for a second or more times against the same harasser or when a victim of sexual harassment lodges a written complaint of sexual harassment.

The UEW sexual harassment policy contains may essential ingredients, its major drawback is its location. It is only available in students handbook. Strategies for publicising and ensuring that all members of the university community have access are weak. For policies to be effective and serve the community, they should include madalities for making thier contents public.

Suggestions for Developing a Sexual Harassment Policy

The dissemination workshops provided occasion to debate the salient features of university-based sexual harassment policies. Research respondents also offered suggestions for managing sexual harassment on the university campuses. The need for a policy to check the occurrence of sexual harassment on the university campuses was affirmed in the research and at all the workshops. Differences in opinions centred more on the form of behaviours that should be sanctioned rather than the need for a sexual harassment policy. The concern was that the image of the universities could be marred by acts of sexual harassment by undermining the universities' educational mission or compromising standards. The policy should aim at creating an environment conducive for academic work.

Workshop participants observed that universities, as institutions for training future leaders and responsible citizens, have a duty to protect individuals within its community and also instil a sense of discipline. The UCC workshop, for example, concluded that the university should show leadership in terms of a commitment to the betterment of the life of its workers by protecting their rights and liberties. In this wise, the universities should re-engineer their policies in a manner that ensures gender sensitivity at all levels of their operations. A possible framework for meeting this objective, it was suggested, was for universities to utilize a framework that positions sexual harassment as a human right violation and an intrusion on the privacy of victims who have to endure embarrassing situation each day. Sexual harassment is discriminatory since it is only females who have to endure *quid pro quo* harassment.

Key Concerns for Managing Sexual Harassment

All the workshops recognized the need for an apex body to take up the responsibility of managing sexual harassment. Such a body will have to be supported by other units established within the office of the Dean of Students and the Counselling Centres. To enhance access, other workshops suggested that interest groups like UTAG, FUSAG, GAUA, TEWU, SRC as well as campus-based religious bodies should have in place a system for receiving sexual harassment complaints. The first point should be any one of the offices identified above. It was recommended that separate offices should be created to deal with complaints from students and staff. Other points of complaints were hall counsellors/tutors or immediate supervisors at the workplaces of staff members who fall victim. The offices of the Vice-Chancellor, the Pro-Vice-chancellor and the Registrar were also assigned varying levels of responsibility in the management system, especially in the area of monitoring.

Participants recognized that investigating sexual harassment complaints is the key to the efficient delivery of justice. The concern of most participants was that the procedure should protect the victim in order to avoid stigmatization. Thus, the number of people involved in the investigation of all sexual harassment cases should be small. Each investigative team should have representatives from the interest groups of the complainant and the accused. The process should avoid delays. One effective means suggested was to provide a procedure for complaints and investigations that was devoid of bureaucratic bottlenecks. Any office that was faced with difficulty investigating a compliant should pass it on to the next higher level office.

Monitoring was recognized as an integral part of the sexual harassment management system and one way of making the delivery of justice effective. The task of monitoring was assigned to bodies such as the investigative team, or units where the complainants belonged. Some workshops, however, recommended a special committee with sole responsibility for monitoring the implementation of decisions from the investigative team. Other systems that could enhance monitoring were provisions for the complainant to petition the investigative team if dissatisfied with the manner in which the complaint is being handled. In addition, the monitoring team should be obliged to submit regular reports to the university authorities.

Suggestions for Preventing Sexual Harassment

Respondents offered suggestions as to how sexual harassment can be prevented on the university campuses. Some felt that it was a question of reducing the incidence of sexual harassment since a total eradication was not possible. Others insisted that managing sexual harassment should focus on changing behaviour. Strategies were suggested that involved empowering vulnerable members of the university community these were either target specific or general to all the vulnerable groups identified. Target specific strategies were mainly directed at students. Workshop participants identified the conception and teaching of courses as an effective media for sensitizing students on sexual harassment. The idea was that all courses should be made gender sensitive and liberal courses on gender be instituted for all students. Other strategies suggested abolishing students' celebrations that were considered obscene and a sustained educational campaign to get members of community to appreciate appropriate values of decent behaviour and abhor obscene behaviour. Students should be involved in formulating rules and regulations on the nature and form that their celebrations should take.

The general strategies outlined to empower vulnerable members of the university community included education designed to change perceptions, and the psychology of sexuality within the university community. There should be sound moral and sex education tailored for harassers. Educational programmes should be undertaken in several ways through periodic programmes such as workshops and seminars for specific target groups in the form of orientation programmes for fresh students and newly-recruited staff. The others should target a larger number of community members through the radio stations on campuses, incorporate sexual harassment messages in official university publications like newsletters, brochures and students handbooks and on billboards.

By way of dealing with the teaching and learning environment that promotes sexual harassment, participants suggested quality assurance in teaching and transparency in the conduct of student examinations and grading systems. A comprehensive code of ethics for all stakeholders should be evolved to address issues such as staff promotions and student grading systems. Improvement in teaching and service delivery in offices and transparency in admissions and room allocation should certainly be of help in promoting a university environment free from sexual harassment. The need to avoid delays in dealing with sexual harassment cases was also suggested.

Participants thought that the most effective means of reaching out to members of the university community was through official channels of the university or through interest groups representation of both official and non-official members of the university communities. These included:

1. The official sections of the university such as the Faculties, Schools, Departments, Units Sections, Halls of Residence, and the Counselling Centres;
2. Interest group representative bodies that had official university recognition like UTAG, GAUA, FUSAG, TEWU, SRC, NUGS, WOMEN'S GROUPS, GRASAG, the Chaplaincy, and the Alumini Associations;
3. Groups that had no official university recognition like the religious groups, ethnic, social and subject associations;
4. Unofficial members of the university community who service the university community like chiefs of village communities; landlords/ladies of private student hostels, transport owner associations (GPRTU), hawkers, and other private service providers.

Sanctioning was identified as an effective preventive strategy and workshop participants suggested that perpetrators should be prosecuted and not just dismissed. There were differences in terms of the factors that should determine the severity of the sanctions. Some believed, for example, that persons in positions of power who sexually bribe or corrupt should be sanctioned in accordance with the positions of responsibility within the university hierarchy. For others, the gravity of the offence committed should determine the nature of the sanction. Some suggested penalties for corrupt behaviours and others believed that students who put up sexually-corrupt behaviours should be counselled. Respondents asked that people who make false allegations should be sanctioned.

Generally the sanctions outlined were varied in intensity. They included:

1. Warnings, reprimands or a letters of apology;
2. Loss of residential status for students, banning the harasser from entering students hall of residence;
3. Fines for students and staff and withholding salary for members of staff;
4. Public exposure of the harasser;
5. Demotion for staff;
6. Dismissal for both staff and students;
7. Legal action with state institutions;
8. Jail sentences for sexual offenders;
9. Castration for rapists.

For those who believed that sexual harassment is a reaction to some provocative behaviour, the solution lay in getting ladies to stop wearing provocative dresses and making demands for favours from their male counterparts. Demands for favours, as explained earlier, were seen as an invitation for some sexual relationship. Favours should be paid back and women can pay back favours they receive from males in one way only, sex. It was suggested that if students could be stopped from mixing with the opposite sex at points on the university campuses termed dubious then the incidence of sexual harassment can be reduced considerably. Managing sexual harassment this way suggests circumscribing female behaviour thus promoting victim blaming.

Suggested Supporting Structures

Participants recommended that the system for managing sexual harassment should be well resourced in order to function effectively. The range of resources identified as necessary were first a comprehensive policy with educational strategies designed to create awareness in the entire university community. Such strategies should be supported by materials like brochures, fliers and billboards, regular university publications like the students' handbooks and newsletters.

In terms of physical facilities, participants mentioned space for counselling and administration as well as equipment in the form of computers and accessories and tape recorders to assist in record keeping and all other administrative work. Other material resource requirements identified were stationery, efficient communication system in the form of telephones, e-mail, mail box and mobile phones for officers. Transport and readily-accessible funds were also identified as material needs.

Human resource needs were identified as skilled personnel who have continuous access to specialized training to enhance the discharge of their duties. Such personnel will be required to carry out functions such as:

1. Investigations;
2. Counselling;
3. Legal advice to the team and victim;
4. Peer counselling system for victims;
5. Discipline;
6. Monitoring;

Other personnel required were secretarial and administrative staff. The personnel of the campus security were recognized as constituting an important component of the sexual harassment management system and will require specialized training to fulfil the demands that will arise. The structures to be set up to support an efficient sexual harassment management system must include those that could help curb the incidence of sexual harassment. An example is a fund for needy students.

Proof of University Commitment

As a first step in showing commitment towards providing an environment free of sexual harassment, participants outlined eight actions that the universities will have to undertake:

1. Setting up a victim support fund;
2. Monitoring cases reported through effective record keeping;
3. Re-engineering university policy by placing emphasis on quality assurance;
4. Providing a slot on the university calendar for observing a gender awareness week;
5. Developing a detailed policy document on sexual harassment
. formulated and approved by the university;
6. Setting up a committee to advise and implement the sexual harassment policy;
7. Creating a gender awareness desk with responsibility for sexual harassment;
8. Providing avenues for publishing findings of an investigative team two weeks after the complaints.

Conclusion

The absence of a policy on sexual harassment and a corresponding structure for handling sexual harassment cases accounted for low levels of reported cases. Setting in place an efficient management system on the university campuses will help to unravel the real incidence of sexual harassment. Major entry points for developing university based on sexual harassment policies include uiversity strategic plans and statutes, which provides the supporting principles. The general details for developing a sexual harassment policy that evolved from the workshops reveal that the campus communities are ready for such a policy and that there exists a strong will to carry the process further. It was recognized that a policy on sexual harassment will have to embrace all members of the university communities. Sexual harassment strategies must be sensitive to the most vulnerable members of the university communities.

Chapter 6

DEVELOPING UNIVERSITY BASED SEXUAL HARASSMENT POLICIES: CHALLENGES AND PROSPECTS

Introduction

Ghanaian universities have always been male-dominated. They only recently attained 30 per cent female-student enrolment. Even though low levels of female participation has been recognized as a problem that merits attention, there are as yet no laid-down strategies to close the gender gap in student enrolment and staff recruitment. Sexual harassment policy offers an opportunity to formally address gender issues systematically on the university campuses. The research findings and the outcome of the dissemination workshops indicate that the need to develop a sexual harassment policy has been realized on all the campuses. What is less clear is how the process should proceed and the contents of the final policy. This chapter examines the implications of the findings of the study discussed in earlier chapters for the development of a sexual harassment policy. It will begin by highlighting important findings of the study and later explore the challenges that the process for developing and implementing a university sexual harassment policy pose.

Highlights

The three categories of respondents covered in the study constitute the main members of the university community. They belonged to different age groups; lecturers were the oldest of the three and students the youngest. Students were the least likely to be married and non-teaching staff most likely to be in consensual relationships. Religious activities engaged respondent's more than professional and social activities. Students spent more time on religious activities than staff; teaching staff were more involved in professional and academic activities than the non-teaching staff and students. The peculiar background of the major members of the university community suggests that other non-university structures can influence decisions and impact perceptions on how sections of the community receive the sexual harassment policy.

The specific experience of sexual harassment and the manner in which it was perceived was gendered on the university campuses. The definition of sexual harassment from the university campuses stressed the sexual content of behaviours as the key element qualifying an action as sexually harassing. Some definitions recognized the subjective interpretation of the act and a few noted the impact of the action. There clearly existed some amount of confusion about sexually-appropriate behaviour. One implication of this confusion revolves around a hazy phenomenon named female promiscuity. This phenomenon identified sometimes as a particular mode of dressing gets blamed as the main cause of sexual harassment on the university campuses.

Several factors affected how behaviours were labelled as sexual harassment on the university campuses. They included the nature and source of the behaviour and also the marital status of the individual at the receiving end. There were sex differences in how sexual harassment was perceived. Respondents were generally more tolerant of gestures and verbal harassment than they were of physical harassment and behaviours that had clear sexual connotations. The prevalent forms of sexual harassment experienced on the campuses were more of those that create a hostile environment like the physical, verbal and non-verbal harassment. The workshops and the field research revealed that the majority of sexual harassment victims are females, especially *quid pro quo* and hostile environment types. Reports of sexual coercion were low. However, male reports of sexual coercion were motivated by same sex harassment suggesting that males were more likely to physically assault each other sexually. Female behaviours that were identified as sexually-harassing for males were those that stimulated their sexual urge or behaviours on the part of females that the males interpreted as invitations to have sex.

The main triggers of sexual harassment identified were those that dwelt on female behaviour like the way women dressed, presented themselves or the places they visited. Male factors identified as sexual harassment triggers were more of their ideas about female sexuality and masculinity. The university environment in terms of pressures of academic work, some forms of celebrations and dwindling access to university facilities, were also noted as important causes of sexual harassment. Generally, respondents felt that females and males were unequal and that work relations within the university were gendered. Further, it was agreed that gender stereotypes feed into work relations in the universities. However the causes of sexual harassment and suggestions offered to curb the incidence of sexual harassment did not question male power. Morality is played up and it becomes the responsibility of females to maintain the appropriate morals defined from a male perspective. The reluctance to question male power in gender relations on the university campuses can lead to scapegoating female behaviour, such as "mode of dressing", "sitting posture", "demands for favours" and "exposure of sexually-sensitive parts" as the cause of sexual harassment which should be targeted in preventive strategies.

Identifying sexual provocation, especially mode of dressing, as sexual harassment presumes that females' choice of clothing will have to be circumscribed. How females dress and what is considered acceptable reinforce the notion that the sexual potential of a woman's body is a key feature of female and male encounters on the university campuses. It is in this light that demands for favours as explained in the third chapter can be seen as a form of sexual harassment. The perception that the female body is a male entitlement and, therefore, its presentation should meet the approval of males raises problems about what should be considered decent dressing. Besides, it reinforces the thinking that favours from males to females have to be returned only through sex.

It is clear that female conception of sex is different from that of males. Two issues come up as a result. One is the woman's dignity and her ability to regulate her sexual behaviour on her own terms. The other is the man's ego conceived as sexual prowess, spelt out as how much sex a man is able to have and where and with which woman and in what circumstances. Clearly, female and male notions of sex are bound to clash and when they do in an environment dominated by perceptions that place women's sexuality at the disposal of men then females will have little control over their sexuality. Respondents' perceptions highlight the power relations among the sexes, particularly the vulnerability of females and how this operates to inform attitudes that feed into sexual harassment on the campuses.

The explanation that sexual provocation is the cause of sexual harassment on the campuses encourages the "blame the victim" attitude and stigmatizes female victims of sexual harassment. Sexual provocation serves as a useful tool for protecting males from accepting the responsibility for their demeaning acts. The force of public shaming which is an important instrument for preventing sexual harassment, is directed at females, the victims, and not males, the perpetrators. Stigmatizing female victims shields male perpetrators.

Developing a University Based Sexual Harassment Policy

The need for a policy on sexual harassment in the university is not in doubt. It is its content and shape that prove challenging. The gender perceptions and dominant notions of masculinity and what is paraded as acceptable female behaviour are heavily tilted against women. The process of developing a university sexual harassment policy presents several challenges, but, as the study revealed, there are several prospects on the various campuses that the process can avail itself of. Reinhart (1999) points out that there is no perfect procedure or perfect policy model for sexual harassment. The environment within which the policy is to be developed and used will determine largely the process and final content of the sexual harassment policy. Initial actions by universities and workplaces in countries such as Australia, the UK and US, where sexual harassment policies were first enacted consisted merely in implementing legislations. Brandt and Too (1999) explain that such measures did not provide infallible solutions and in no time institutions and universities realized the need to redraft their policies to take into account other forms of discrimination and greater collaboration with other legal authorities. An effective sexual harassment policy should be based on a clear and broad framework that enables a critical appraisal of the peculiar problems on each campus.

Initiating the Process

An ILO survey of leading business institutions and sexual harassment revealed that these companies set out policies to address sexual harassment in their work places for several reasons. These reasons include the need to cut down on the cost suffered by companies in payment of compensation and administrative cost responding to legal action associated with sexual harassment (Reinhart, 1999). Other reasons were the need to apply ethical principles of treating every employee with dignity and respect. Some companies believed that reducing the impact of sexual harassment on productivity can help boost the image of the company as gender sensitive (*ibid*).

Critical steps in the development of sexual harassment policy begin first with an identification of the need to have such a policy and determining what legal provisions especially at the national level should be the point of reference. There are several reasons why universities should have sexual harassment policies. The Ghanaian Constitution of 1992 provides a useful legal basis for developing a sexual harassment policy. Statutes and strategic plans in all the universities contain provisions that lend support to the constitutional provisions and these can be used to set the tone and offer justification for the policy. The workshops believed, for example, that a good sexual harassment policy will enhance the image of the universities. Respondents also acknowledged the need for the universities to play leadership role in creating work and educational environments that are gender sensitive.

Universities have a responsibility to protect the dignity of their members and ensure that in the discharge of their duties they are free to interact and benefit from their stay on the campus without fear of sexual harassment. The suggestion of the workshops that sexual harassment should be positioned as a human rights violation as well as a question of equal opportunity because it constitutes an intrusion on the privacy and dignity of the individual is valid and worth considering, for sexual harassment affects women unequally.

The question of determining who should be involved in the development of the policy is a key concern that all universities will have to address. The workshops suggested equal representation for both females and males on the committee. The selection of the team should be done in close consultation with all representative groups who should be given a free hand to select their own members. The credibility and representativeness of the team will enhance the ownership of the policy as well as its ability to protect and promote the rights of women. The workshops have already identified key university groups like interest group representative bodies.

The Content of a Sexual Harassment Policy
An ILO report on combatting workplace sexual harassment recommends that sexual harassment policies should include fair main components. These are first a policy statement which situates the policy and highlights

its underlying principles and concepts. The other three are the complaints procedure, disaplinary rules and a training and communications strategy (ILO 1992). Once the components of the policy have been set out, attention should be paid to its general orientation. a sexual harassment policy can be effective if it is gender sensitive nd opens out to other related issues like code of ethics and anti-discrimination policies. The content of the policy should be designed therefore to promote gender sensitivity and protect the rights and dignity of female members of the university communities.

The workshops acknowledged the need for a university sexual harassment policy to be informed by the preventive approach so that academic discourse can take place without undermining the principles of academic freedom and critical thinking. To this end, a sexual harassment policy should be placed in the broader framework of a gender policy that covers all activities on the university campuses. Sexual harassment can also be positioned within equal opportunity laws or become the focus of university code of behaviour.

An examination of sexual harassment policies of some universities reveals similarities in terms of the format adopted (eg. some universities in Botswana, Australia, South Africa, Canada, Sweden and US). Generally, these policies have been enacted on their own or incorporated into policies on gender, sexual offences, and code of ethics or equal opportunity. Their underlying principles are rights-based with an attempt to situate the problem and provide information on its occurrence, prevalence within the university or the rest of the country. The policies also state the position of the university on sexual harassment. The supporting university, national, and international statutes or legislation as well as relevant policies are explained.

A sexual harassment policy should give occasion to discuss a code of conduct for all sections of the university community. The debate on sexual harassment strays into other areas of comportment and as a result generates difficulties in terms of isolating what is sexually appropriate and what is sexually-harassing. Issues that border on the abuse of rights and discrimination on the university campuses will have to be discussed. A policy on sexual harassment should open up other areas, such as code of ethics and equal opportunity for all sections of the university community. The policy should reinforce the equal rights of all members of the university community, indicate clearly that sexual harassment is an offence and that the university aims through the policy to reinforce its commitment to promoting and protecting the rights of all to equal participation in all its activities.

The fact that sections of university community perceive sexual provocation as sexual harassment has several implications. The first is the notion of sexuality, what is perceived as acceptable sexual behaviour and who bears responsibility for unacceptable sexual behaviour. The second, which derives from the first, is the forms of behaviour that will be identified as sexual harassment. The third, the implicit assumption that is not being questioned is that males sexualize all their relations with women. The notions of masculinity held by both females and males make sexual harassment a just reaction to inappropriate female behaviour. As a result the "appropriate" expression of masculinity becomes a justification to sexually harass a "provocative" female. Some ambiguity arises here that needs to be cleared before an appropriate policy can be developed. It has to do with what males call sexually-harassing and how it constitutes a just cause to harass females. This attitude presents a real challenge to efforts aimed at promoting and protecting female rights through a sexual harassment policy.

Chapter 3 noted the general perception on the university campuses that the defining element is the sexual intention of an act and therefore its content. Few were concerned about the interpretation of the harassed or its possible impact. Non-teaching staff gave a wider interpretation of sexual harassment. This constitutes perhaps a reflection of the need for them to mark the boundaries between sexual relations between mutually-consenting adults and sexual manipulations in their work environment. Extra marital sexual relationships between members of the university community especially with unequal institutional power present a dilemma since they offer a potential avenue for sexual corruption and favouritism. In the face of dwindling university resources access to university resources gets more restricted and conditions for fulfilling university requirements for academic and occupational progression become more demanding. Sexual harassment policy will have to address these forms of liaisons and offer some regulations.

The credibility of the policy and its effectiveness depend on effective consultation and education about sexual harassment as a human rights and gender issue. The content of the policy should specify the commitment of the university. The definition of sexual harassment developed to guide the policy should be clear and unambiguous about what is sexual harassment and more importantly that no form of it will be tolerated within the university. All members should be aware of the complaints and investigative procedures. The policy should state clearly which behaviours will be sanctioned.

Implementing the Policy

Each university should appoint a body with sole responsibility for implementing the sexual harassment policy. The responsibilities and powers of this body should be specified. The apex body should be responsible for receiving complaints, investigating and implementing recommendations of the investigating teams and monitoring compliance and providing education on sexual harassment. This body, as suggested by the workshops, should be supported by smaller units set up in faculties, schools and institutes and they should all be properly resourced with adequate financial, material and human resources. The peculiar circumstances and operating structures on the campuses will determine to a large extent where to place the supporting structures. All members of the university community should have easy access to some facility to lodge complaints. Access can be further enhanced by incorporating offices of interest groups within the structures for receiving complaints.

Complaints and Investigative Procedures. The nature of the experience of sexual harassment calls for a complaints procedure which is different from the normal grievance procedures (Reinhart, 1999; AWLA, 2003). Victims of sexual harassment, we noted in Chapter 4, were reluctant to make complaints because they often fear victimization particularly where their alleged harassers were in positions of authority or felt embarrassed by the demeaning nature of the experience and the resulting stigmatization they will attract. The AWLA Ghana (2003) checklist notes that sexual harassment is a sensitive issue to the investigator as well. The challenge is to develop a complaints procedure which responds to all needs and inspires confidence.

There are basically two forms of procedure depending on the nature and frequency of occurrence of the sexually-harassing experience. The informal procedure which consists of an oral complaint recognizes the fact that most victims just want the harassment to stop and are put off by having to make a written complaint (Reinhart, 1999). In Chapter 5, we noted that most people preferred reporting their sexual harassment experiences to non-sanctioning sections of the university like the counselling centre. An informal complaint especially to a confidential counsellor or an ombudsperson creates confidence because of the emotional support offered by the confidential counsellor. The informal procedure involves fewer people it is faster, and less costly. The ILO study discovered that companies using the informal procedure will often use mediation to resolve the complaint in the following four instances.

1. The beginning of the process;
2. If the complainant chooses this option;
3. If the harassment is not a long-standing problem and;
4. If the alleged harasser seems open to discussion (Reinhart, 1999).

The formal procedure as described in the UEW report involves a written complaint by the complainant which is sent to an identifiable person who is required to undertake a confidential investigation of the case within a specified short period. The units involved are carefully selected to offer the complainant support and assure all the parties involved that they will be treated fairly. Here too, the complainant is represented by an official who is assigned by the university or chosen for the purpose by the complainant.

There are no standard procedures or limits to what an acceptable formal procedure should be. A few factors noted in the ILO report (Reinhart, 1999) as well as the AWLA Ghana (2003) checklist are worth considering here;

1. First, every single procedure should be determined more by the persons involved and the wishes of the complainant;
2. Relatively simple procedures inspire confidence and encourage more people to use the system to seek redress;
3. All sides of each case should be taken into consideration and conclusions should be drawn only when the whole story has been established;
4. The procedure should be fast and inspire confidence in all thus reinforcing the commitment of the institution to a

harassment free environment;

5. Lines of authority and responsibilities of key officers should be clearly defined and;
6. All complainants should be protected from their powerful harassers.

The AWLA Ghana (2003) checklist developed as a guide for good practice on sexual harassment in the workplace states that "the right to file a complaint includes the right to expect a speedy response and the right to an efficient system of justice administration . . . the investigative mechanism should ensure effective, efficient and supportive neutral response to the complainant of sexual harassment". In Chapter 5, the importance of the structures set up to investigate sexual harassment complaints to the efficient delivery of justice was underscored. Cases of sexual harassment should be investigated properly and documented without delay. The complainant should be protected from stigmatization through the promotion of strict confidentiality during the investigation. The rights of all involved in the case should be respected i.e. the rights of both the complainant and alleged harasser. This will ensure that all involved respect the outcome of the conclusion of the investigation. The investigative procedure should be simple and uphold the suggestion of the workshops to be devoid of cumbersome bureaucratic procedures.

The representation on each investigative team should be clearly specified in the policy. The sexual harassment policy of the University of Botswana for example provides special training for all members of the team. Others like the Antioch College Policy, in addition to providing training, states the duration of membership as well as the tenure of the board. In addition, provision is made for the complainant to be represented and care is taken to ensure that the alleged harasser also has support. The accused and the complainant all have a right of appeal should they happen to find the conclusions of the team unsatisfactory.

Education and Training. Education and training constitute important components of the sexual harassment policy because they help to promote acceptability of the policy. Regular schedules for education and training should be built into the policy. Education should aim at providing information about the contents of the policy and the definition of sexual harassment and identify the types of behaviours that will not be tolerated.

Education should make members of the university communities sensitive to sexual harassment as a problem and give all a clear understanding of their rights and responsibilities. Education should aim at preventing sexual harassment by changing attitudes and behaviours, giving greater self assurance to vulnerable members and making sexual harassment illegal.

In Chapter 4, we noted that the experience of sexual harassment on the university campuses was gendered in its sources, form and target. Major causes of sexual harassment mentioned pointed to male power buttressed by position of authority within the university structures. An important starting point for education and training within the policy, therefore becomes gender sensitization for all sections of the university community. Gender issues should look more to gender relations and how they are structured and less to adding women on to sectors where they are underrepresented. Women are not by nature gender concious so adding women on without the required sensitization cannot provide the needed impact rather they might buttress the *status quo*. Gender sensitization is important for enhancing the development of an accurate definition of sexual harassment and what behaviours should be sanctioned. Gender sensitization should also aim at changing perceptions about masculinity which encourage blaming females for the sexual harassment they suffer. Education should lead to a re-conception of female sexuality that gives women greater control over the expressions of their sexuality and also provide measures designed to compensate for individual deficiencies, for example, by improving the capacity of individuals to manage their sexuality creatively without exploiting other notions that should be targeted are perceptions about gender notes which encourage victim blaming.

Education and training should provide information about what to do when sexually harassed or when faced with a case of sexual-harassment. Special training should be designed for all involved in developing or implementing and monitoring the policy. The content of training should cover principles of human rights and gender relations and supporting structures of female subordination. Members involved in receiving and investigating complaints will need additional training in principles of investigating sexual harassment complaints and how to assess credibility in cases of sexual harassment.

The liability of the universities extends beyond recognized members to those who provide services to the university communities like landlords and landladies of hostels where students reside, shop owners and transport operators (AWLA Ghana, 2003). All service providers should be informed about the content of as well as their rights and responsibilities within the policy. Training must highlight measures in the policy that hold members accountable for their behaviours by specifying the rewards for those who promote the policy (Reinhart, 1999).

Education and training should utilize several media in order to reach all members of the university community. The five media suggested in Chapter 5 are repeated here:

1. Orientation programmes for fresh students and newly-recruited staff;
2. Special workshops and seminars for staff members;
3. Radio programmes on campus radio stations;
4. Official university publications like newsletters, brochures, students handbooks;
5. Special billboards and all university notice boards.

Other measures beyond education and training are required to strengthen and give greater power to the vulnerable members and remove conditions on the university campuses that promote sexual harassment. These include gendering all university courses and giving a different orientation to student celebrations. There should be transparency in grading students' work, staff recruitment and promotion, as well as the allocation of university resources like student accommodation. The conduct of student examinations and grading of student work should attract greater transparency than it does at present. Students, for example, should see all their marked examination scripts and lecturers should be available to explain to student why they obtained a certain grade just as it is done for class work. The universities should put a ceiling on the student-staff ratio beyond which additional students will not be admitted. The present practice of increasing student intake suggests that university authorities assume that their institutions together with the staff and the surrounding communities have some elastic capacity to absorb any number of students. The assumption requires a scietific investigation to establish the real capacity of both human and physical resources that the universities utilise.

Sanctioning and Monitoring Compliance. The mechanisms put in place for sanctioning harassers should promote confidence and encourage members of the university community to utilize provisions within the policy to enhance their participation in university activities. Once investigation proves that sexual harassment has occurred, the alleged harasser will have to be disciplined. Sanctions should be timely and appropriate to the offence and should be in line with what has been spelt out in the policy. Sanctioning should be instituted for harassers who attempt to intimidate a complainant during investigation and for the complainant where allegations prove to be intentionally false. The policy should include provisions for monitoring compliance and evaluating the successes and constraints of the measures set out to implement the policy.

Conclusion

The peculiar character of Ghanaian public universities and their strategic location within the socio-economic structure of the country call for greater attention to sexual harassment and measures for enhancing female participation in the public space. The study confirmed that sexual harassment was a gender issue in the manner in which it was experienced and conceived on the university campuses. The struggle to separate sexual harassment from morality placed the blame on female for events that demeaned them and promoted forms of masculinity that was punitive of female expression of sexuality that was considered immoral. In all, females carried an unfair share of the blame for the occurrence of sexual harassment on the campuses. Developing a sexual harassment policy should confront broader gender considerations. The supporting legal provisions as provided by the Ghanaian Constitution, the Labour (Act 561) and the statutes of the universities are indeed important starting points. The right type of education and training buttressed by adequate and meaningful consultation will ensure that the final sexual harassment policies that are developed on each campus will serve their purpose, help to tackle issues of gender discrimination and help to affirm all these universities as equal opportunity centres they claim to be.

NOTES

1. UTAG is the representative body of teaching staff in Ghanaian universities.

2. Student Representative Councils are university-campus-based student organizations.

3. NUGS is a national-based organization of students in tertiary institutions in Ghana.

4. FUSSAG is a national organization of senior non-teaching staff in Ghanaian universities.

5. GAUA as the name suggests is made up of top-level uni ersity administrators.

6. TEWU is an affiliate of the Trades Union Congress (Ghana). All university junior non-teaching staff are members.

7. In 2003, UEW attained the status of a full-fledged university and its name changed from the University College of Education, Winneba.

8. See Prah's presentation on "Sexual harassment in Ghana", *Dissemination Workshop Report UCC* April 7, 2003.

9. See *Dissemination Workshop Report* (UEW) [May 26, 2003].

10. See *Dissemination Workshop Report* (UCC) [April 7, 2003].

11. See *Dissemination Workshop Report* (UEW) [May 26, 2003].

12. See presentation by Kuffour in the KNUST *Dissemination Workshop Report* 22, April 2003.

13. See presentation by Tete-Mensah in the UEW Dissemination Workshop Report [26, May 2003].

14. Twi translated literally as "make me bankrupt" a situation in which males show off by spending a lot of money on females.

15. Another Twi word meaning "Pamper me".

16. See UG *Dissemination Workshop Report* 10, April 2003.

17. See *Dissemination Workshop Report* UDS April 24, 2003

18. See *Dissemination Workshop Reports* UDS and UEW.

APPENDICES

Targeted, Achieved Sample Size And Response Rate

CATEGORYOF RESPONDENTS	SEX	TARGETED	ACHIEVED	RESPONSE RATE
	Female	1071	779	72.7
Students	Male	1071	646	60.3
	Total	**2142**	**1425**	**66.5**
	Female	201	73	36.3
Teaching Staff	Male	201	144	71.6
	Total	*402*	*217*	*54.0*
	Female	343	237	69.1
Non-Teaching Staff	Male	343	225	65.6
	Total	*686*	*462*	*67.3*
	Female	45	30	66.7
Key Persons	Male	45	41	91.1
	Total	*90*	*71*	*78.9*
	Female	1660	1119	67.4
TOTAL	Male	1660	1056	63.6
	Total	*3320*	*2175*	*65.5*

Source: Field Data 2001

APPENDIX 2
Total Study Population

	STUDENTS			TEACHING STAFF			NON-TEACHING			TOTAL		
	Female	Male	All	Female	Male	All	Female	Male	All	Female	Male	All
UCC	2,336	6,623	8,959	27	228	255	359	1,576	1,935	2,722	8,427	11,149
UCEW	1,885	4,153	6,038	28	206	234	142	493	635	2,055	4,852	6,907
UDS	113	594	707	8	108	116	*	*	298	#121	#702	1,121
UG	5,334	9,340	14,674	115	464	579	693	2,769	3,462	6,142	12,573	18,715
KNUST	2,192	8,141	10,333	33	436	469	418	1,888	2,306	2,643	10,465	13,108
TOTAL	11,860	28,851	40,711	211	1,442	1,653	–	–	8,636	#12,071	#30,293	51,000

*Female/male figures were not available

#Calculations based on figures for the four universities whose female/male figures were available.

Source: University Basic Statistics; University of Cape Coast 2000.
University Basic Statistics; University College of Education, Winneba 2000.
University Basic Statistics; University of Ghana 2000.
University Basic Statistics; University for Development Studies 2000.
University Basic Statistics; Kwame Nkrumah University of Science & Technology 2000.

APPENDIX 3

Total Number of Workshop Participants

Category	KNUST			UCC			UDS			UEW			UG			TOTAL		
	F	M	T	F	M	T	F	M	T	F	M	T	F	M	T	F	M	T
Students	10	11	21	5	30	35	1	17	18			14	8	4	12			101
Teaching	8	11	19	8	24	32	1	4	5			11	10	6	16			83
Non-teaching	8	13	21	8	7	15	24	10	34			20	10	8	18			108
TOTAL	26	35	61	21	61	82	26	31	57	20	26	46	28	18	46	108	184	292

APPENDIX 4

DATA GATHERING INSTRUMENTS

Questionaire For Students

We are from the Centre for Development Studies, University of Cape Coast. We are conducting a study on sexual harassment in Ghanaian public universities. The study seeks to investigate the incidence, nature and forms of sexual harassment as exists on the university campuses in Ghana. You have been randomly selected to be part of the study. Your response to the questions about to be posed to you will provide vital information for the eventual development of an effective framework for managing sexual harassment in this university. The information you give us will be kept confidential; no one will ever know what you said. We will like to crave your indulgence and co-operation for your time as you answer these questions.

Time interview started
SECTION 1 Respondent's Background
We will like to begin by asking you questions about yourself.
1.1   Sex 1. Female   2. Male
1.2   Religion 1. Christianity   2. Islamic   3. Traditional
        4. No religion   5. Others (specify) ....
1.3   Residential Status   1. Residential   2. Non residential
1.4   Nationality ....
1.5   Educational Background (highest level attained)
        1. None   2. Non formal   3. Elementary/JSS
        4. Vocational   5. Secondary/Technical   6. Training College
        7. Polytechnic   8. University   9. Other Tertiary (Specify) ....
1.6   Mother's occupation
1.7   Mother's education
        1. None   2. Non formal   3. Elementary/JSS 4. Vocational
        5. Secondary/Technical   6.Training College 7.Polytechnic
        8. University   9. Other Tertiary (Specify) ....
1.8   Father's occupation
1.9   Father's education   1. None 2. Non formal 3. Elementary/JSS
        4. Vocational   5. Secondary/Technical 6. Training College

7. Polytechnic 8. University 9. Other Tertiary (Specify) ....
1.10 In what year did you enter this university? ....
1.11 What course of study are you pursuing in this university? ....
1.12 In what year and month were you born year [........] month [..........]
1.13 At what age were you admitted into this university? ....
1.14 Marital Status 1. Married 2. Single 3. Divorced
4. Widowed 5. Separated 6. Consensual
1.15 Do you have a boy/girl friend on campus? 1. Yes 2. No
1.16 Would you say that this is a friend you are very close to or just a casual friend? 1. very close 2. Casual
1.17 Is this friend a student? 1. Yes 2. No
1.18 Are you a member of any type of group or association or organization which meets regularly (Tick appropriate column)

Associations	On-Campus	Off-Campus
Social grouping		
Political grouping		
Ethnic grouping		
Academic grouping		
Professional grouping		
Other (specify)		

SECTION 2 Defining sexual harassment and setting limits
2.1 What to you constitutes sexual harassment?
2.2 Which behaviours will you classify as sexual harassment?
2.3 How do people here generally define sexual harassment?
2.4 What behaviours do people here generally describe as sexual harassment?

SECTION 3 Attitudes About Sexual Harassment
People in the university community find themselves in situations where they get easily sexually harassed. Some people believe that sexual harassment can be avoided and some people get sexually harassed because they invited it on themselves. Some people also believe that sexual harassment is an alien concept and most of the things people label as sexual harassment are culturally acceptable in Ghana. Which of the following acts do you think are unacceptable and should carry the name sexual harassment

3.1   Verbal abuse about sexual habits by a colleague or peer [...]
3.2   Sexist remarks about a woman's body [...]
3.3   Sexist remarks about a woman's clothing [...]
3.4   Sexist remarks about a woman's sexual habits [...]
3.5   Subtle pressure for sex [...]
3.6   Suggestive gestures alluding to sex [...]
3.7   Lurid jokes about sex to females [...]
3.8   Uninvited touching, [...]
3.9   Uninvited patting, pinching [...]
3.10   Uninvited fondling [...]
3.11   Uninvited rubbing grabbing, [...]
3.12   Uninvited kissing, [...]
3.13   Demand for sexual favours under a veiled threat for a job or academic favours [...]

SECTION 4 Causes/Sources

4.1 Here is a list of factors that have been noted to promote sexual harassment in other universities. Which of these factors are likely to attract sexual harassment on campus here? You can give 1 to the factor you consider most likely to attract sexual harassment and 2 to the next and so on.

— Admissions into programmes in the university   [...]
— A basis for offering some form of academic support   [...]
— Passing end of semester examinations   [...]
— Getting a good grade in examinations   [...]
— When some females want to contest high office on campus [...]

4.2   What factors do you think encourage some people to harass others?
4.3   How will you explain the occurrence of sexual harassment in this university?
4.4   Admissions into some programmes of the university are generally believed to attract more instances of sexual harassment than others.
        1. Yes   2. No
4.5   Please explain your answer.
4.6   The balance between the sexes in a particular department can encourage sexual harassment.   1. Yes 2. No
4.7   Which of the following balance is the cause of sexual harassment in the section/department that you belong to?
        1. Females are too few   2. Males are too few
        3. Too many males   4. Too many females
4.8   Sexual harassment is used to deter females from holding high office in this university.   1. Yes   2. No

SECTION 5 Assumptions about Sexual Harassment

5.1 Who do you think is more likely to be sexually harassed?
1. Females   2. Males

5.2 Explain your answer.

5.3 Do females and males have the same experience of sexual harassment?
1. Yes   2. No

5.4 Do males also experience sexual harassment? 1. Yes   2. No

5.5 What behaviours do men generally consider as sexually harassing?

5.6 What behaviours do females generally consider as sexual harassment?

5.7 Do you believe that some behaviour of women generally have the tendency to invite sexual harassment?   1. Yes   2. No

5.8 Explain your answer.

5.9 Can females adopt behaviours that can ward off sexual harassment?
1. Yes   2. No

5.10 Explain your answer. ....

5.11 Can people adopt behaviours that will enable them ward off sexual harassment?   1. Yes   2. No

5.12 Explain your answer. ....

5.13 Do males sexually harass other males? 1. Yes 2. No

5.14 Explain your answer. ....

5.15 In what ways can males sexually harass other males?

5.16 In what ways can females sexually harass males?

5.17 Members of the university community most likely to suffer sexual harassment

Categories	Code	Explain
Categories of males most likely to face harassment from females		
Categories of males most likely to face harassment from males		
Categories of females most likely to face harassment from females		
Categories of females most likely to face harassment from males		

Code 1. Students   2. Lectures   3. Teaching Assistants
      4. Senior Staff   5. Junior Staff   6. Others (Landlords, etc,)

5.18 Which department/section of the university community is sexual harassment most likely occur?

SECTION 6. Female/Male Experience of Sexual Harassment

Please specify you what you think about the following statements by indicating whether you strongly agree (SA), agree (A), disagree (D), or strongly disagree (SDA) in the boxes provided

		SA	A	D	SDA
6.1	More women than men face haressment				
6.2	Women will not be sexually harassed if they learnt to behave themselves				
6.3	Women generally face harassment because of the way they dress				
6.4	It is only a certain type of woman who gets harassed				
6.5	Women generally can prevent sexual harassment if they resisted male sexually advances hard enough				
6.6	Most of the time when women say no they mean yes men only have to press hard				
6.7	Some females are not offended by sexually harassing events they even enjoy them				
6.8	Female who learn to keep away from certain places do not suffer sexual harassment				
6.9	Some females only exaggerate and even tell lies about being sexually harassed				
6.10	It is only a certain type of person who sexually harass others				
6.11	Males who harass others are sick or ill or even under some form of stress				
6.12	Complementing a woman does not constitute sexual harassment				
6.13	Most women who experience sexual harassment ask for it				

	SA	A	D	SDA
6.14 Female students who engage in commercial sex are more likely to be sexually harassed				
6.15 Once a student is involved in commercial sex she should not complain if she finds herself being sexually harassed				
6.16 The body language and attitudes of women tends to invite sexual harassment from males				
6.17 Some people take advantage of certain circumstances to sexually harass others				
6.18 Some people behave in a certain way in order to avoid being sexually harassed				

SECTION 7. Personal Experience of Sexual Harassment
The next batch of questions cover an area that might bring some discomfort for you. Ever so often in our lives we do have experiences that tend to be painful or embarrassing. The questions cover ways in which people harass other people and possible ways you might have been harassed yourself. Please do try to be as open as and truthful as possible. As you are already aware the answers you provide will be treated as secrets and no one will ever know that you have said anything.

7.1 Have you ever had any experience that you consider sexually harassing?
 1. Yes 2. No
7.2 Please describe any such experience/s you have had which you consider sexually harassing.
7.3 How often do you face this kind of experience? (Please state number of times within a week or month etc.)
7.4 Where did this experience occur? ....
7.5 Who are the perpetrators? Please indicate sex............ rank........... and position or status of the perpetrators (name not required)
7.6 When was the last time you had such an experience? ....
7.7 What do you think was the cause of the harassment? ....
7.8 What was your reaction?..
7.9 What effect did the harassment have on you? . ...
7.10 Who did you report to? ....
7.11 What action was taken? ....
7.12 Were you satisfied with the type of action taken? 1. Yes 2. No
7.13 Explain your answer. ....

7.14   Why did you refuse to report if you did not report your experience to any one?

7.15   Do you find your self being continuously harassed
   1.   By the same group of people?   [...]
   2.   By a particular person?   [...]

7.16   Indicate the person or group of persons most likely to harass you.
   ....

7.17   What behaviours of yours generally have been interpreted as an invitation to harass you?

7.18   Do you generally experience any of the following? If you do indicate the source of the experience and how often it happens to you in a week/ month/year as well as where it occurs

Experience	Source *(Type of person)*	Location *(Place)*	Frequency *(No. of times)*
Unwanted touching	....	....	....
Cat calls	....	....	....
Rubbing	....	....	....
Booing and jeers	....	....	....
Kissing & grabbing	....	....	....
Name calling	....	....	....
Fondling	....	....	....
Teasing	....	....	....
Exposure to pornography	....	....	....
Sexual jokes	....	....	....

7.19   Has any one hinted that you could lose your job or that your work might be hurt if you did not meet some demands like a date or sex?
   1. Yes   2. No

7.20   Please explain. ....

7.21   Has any teacher/lecturer ever hinted or threatened that you could fail your exams or get bad marks or that your schooling would be damaged if you did not meet some sexual demand like sex or a data?
   1. Yes   2. No

7.22   Describe the circumstance. ....

7.23   As a child did anyone at school ever give you any attention you considered sexual that made you uncomfortable?   1. Yes
   2. No

7.24   Describe the circumstance. ....

7.25   Has any man ever forced or persuaded you to have sex against your will by threatening, holding you down or hurting you in some way?
1. Yes   2. No

7.26   When did this happen to you? ....

7.27   Has any one insisted that you meet some demand for a date or sex before you would offer of admission in this university?
1. Yes   2. No

7.28   Explain the circumstance. ....

7.29   Do you know of any one who has experienced sexual harassment?
1. Yes   2. No

7.30   Sex........... position............. and department............ of person

7.31   What was the nature of this experience? ....

7.32   Who did the person report the experience to? ....

7.33   Why?...

7.34   What action was taken? ....

7.35   Was the person who suffered the harassment satisfied with the action?
1. Yes   2. No

7.36   What did the person do? ....

7.37   What would you have done if it were you? ....

7.38   Have you ever reported any experience of sexual harassment that you had to any one? 1. Yes   2. No

7.39   Who did you report to?..

7.40   Why? ....

7.41   How long have you been experiencing sexual harassment before you decided to report?

7.42   What made you decide to report to the body/person you reported to? ....

7.43   What action was taken by body/person you reported to? ....

7.44   What action were you advised to take? ....

7.45   What action did you take? ....

7.46   What sanctions did the person harassing you get? ....

7.47   Were you happy about the disciplinary action taken? 1. Yes 2. No

7.48   If you had to decide what punishment the person should get what would you decide?

7.49   Did you withdraw the charges after reporting? 1. Yes 2. No

7.50   Why did you withdraw the charges? ....

7.51   Did any one threaten or put pressure on you to withdraw the charges?
1. Yes   2. No

7.52   If yes, explain what happened. ....

7.53   Have you ever discussed with any one about your harassment?
1. Yes   2. No

7.54   Who did you discuss your experience with? ....

7.55   Did you seek for help? 1. Yes   2. No

7.56   Explain your answer. ....

7.57   Did any one intervene on your behalf to end the harassing experience?
       1. Yes 2. No

7.58   Who did? Position and rank of person (Name not required) ....

7.59   If you had a sexually harassing problem who would you feel comfortable
       talking to?

7.60   As a child did anyone at school ever give you any attention you
       considered sexual that made you uncomfortable?   1. Yes
       2. No

7.61   If yes how often was this experience? ....

7.62   Who (rank/position and relationship to you) gave you this attention?
       ....

7.63   What was your reaction? ....

7.64   Why did you react in this way?..

SECTION 8. Impact

8.1   If you have experienced sexual harassment describe the effect it had on
       you.

8.2   Were others around you affected by the experience? 1. Yes   2. No

8.3   If yes in what ways were they affected by your experience/how were
       they affected?

8.4   If you know of someone who has experienced sexual harassment describe
       the effect it had on this person. ....

8.5   Does the knowledge that some colleague is facing sexual harassment
       affect you and other colleagues?   1. Yes   2. No

8.6   Explain your answer. ....

8.7   Are some people compelled to tolerate sexual harassment because of the
       fear that they might lose some academic or professional favour?
       1. Yes   2. No

8.8   How far is it true that if one does not give in to sexual advances in this
       university one's career advancement might be compromised.
       ....

8.9   Are people here generally able to defy the odds and reject sexual
       harassment despite the problems their action might pose for their own
       career? 1. Yes   2. No

8.10   Explain. Does the fear of going through a sexually harassing experience
       ever intimidate you?   1. Yes 2. No

8.11   Please explain your answer. ....

SECTION 9. Finance Expenditure
9.1   What do you need money for on this campus? ....
9.2   How do students meet their financial needs? (Source of funding)
       1. SSNIT loan   2. Parents 3. Boy/girl friend
       4. Other (specify) ....
9.3   Who provides for your financial needs whilst on campus (just state the
       relationship to the one name not required) ....
9.4   Do you expect that your partner provides you with some form of support
       for your financial needs on campus? 1. Yes   2. No
9.5   Explain your answer. ....
9.6   In what ways do students in their attempt to meet their financial needs
       fall prey to sexual harassment?

SECTION 10. Sexual habits; Sexuality and Commercial Sex
10.1   Do you think that it is proper for female to have sex with someone she is
       not married to?   1. Yes 2. No
10.2   Explain your answer. ....
10.3   Do you think that it is proper for a male to have sex with someone he is
       not married to?   1. Yes   2. No
10.4   Explain your answer. ....
10.5   Do you think that when females say no to sexual advances they really
       mean no?   1. Yes 2. No
10.6   Explain your answer. ....
10.7   Does the fact that a relationship is going steady entitle a boy to have sex
       with his girl friend any time he feels like it?   1. Yes   2. No
10.8   Explain your answer. ....

SECTION 11. Making Sexual Harassment Visible
11.1   In your opinion do think that the number of cases of sexual harassment
       that we get to hear about is a true reflection of the amount of sexual
       harassment cases that are experienced on this campus? 1. Yes   2. No
11.2   Why do you say that? ....
11.3   Do you think that all who experience sexual harassment report their
       experience? 1. Yes   2. No
11.4   If not why do you think that people are not reporting their experience of
       sexual harassment?
11.5   If you do experience sexual harassment would you prefer that the person
       you talk to comes from the
       1. Same ethnic group   2. Religious group   3. Social group
       4. Political group
11.6   Why? ....

11.7   If you did experience sexual harassment would you prefer that the person you talked to comes from the
1. Same ethnic group   2. Religious group   3. Social group
4. Political group
11.8   Explain your answer. ....

SECTION 12. The University Regulatory System
12.1   Do you know of any rules/regulations within the university for dealing specifically with sexual harassment?   1. Yes   2. No
12.2   If yes what is it? ....
12.3   Where can this rules and regulations be found? ....
12.4   What sections/departments are responsible for handling sexual harassment?
12.5   Have you ever had to use the services of the section or departments responsible for handling sexual harassment?   1. Yes   2. No
12.6   If yes state the particular unit that you used. ....
12.7   Were you satisfied with the assistance you received? 1. Yes   2. No
12.8   Would you use this system again if you had a similar experience?
1. Yes   2. No
12.9   Explain your answer? ....
12.10 Would you recommend this system to any one who has a sexual harassment problem?   1. Yes   2. No
12.11 Explain your answer? ....

SECTION 13. Group Dynamism and Sexual Harassment
Please specify you what you think about the following statements by indicating whether you strongly agree (SA=4), agree (A=3), disagree (D=2), strongly disagree (SDA=1) in the boxes provided

	SA	A	D	SDA
13.1 It is not right to report a sexual harassment offence perpetrated by someone from your own tribe knowing that the person might lose his/her education?	·			
13.2 Some girls have a habit of accusing some people from some religious groups or ethnic groups as likely harassers.				
13.3 Some girls likely to be victims of harassment because they belong to a particular ethnic or religious group				

	SA	A	D	SDA
13.4 If members of a disciplinary team belong to the same ethnic/religious group as you then you will be more likely to receive a fair hearing at in a sexual harassment suit				
13.5 People generally will not report their experience of sexual harassment because a member of their tribe/ethnic group might lose his/her education				
13.6 Some people have a habit of accusing some people of sexually harassing them because those people belong to a particular ethnic/ religious group				
13.7 Some members of some ethnic group are more likely to harass women because of the way females are valued in their ethnic group				
13.8 The way women are presented in some cultures makes them easy prey for sexual harassers				
13.9 Some people are likely to be victims of harassment because they belong to a particular ethnic/religious group				
13.10 If members of a disciplinary team belonged to the same ethnic/religious group as you will you be more likely to receive a fair hearing in a sexual harassment case				

SECTION 14. Conclusion

14.1 What do you think should be done to end sexual harassment in this university?

14.2 Is there anything else that you will want to say about the sexual harassment that this interview did not cover?..

14.3 Before we finish can you say a few words about what you thought about the subject that we have just discussed? ....

14.4 Were all the issues that you thought are important to sexual harassment in this university covered in this interview? 1. Yes 2. No

14.5 What additional comments do you have to make about this interview?

14.6 Do you think that there are a lot of these kinds of problems in this area? 1. Yes 2. No

14.7 Explain your answer.
....

14.8 Do you think people would come out and talk about their sexually harassing experience to researchers in this study? 1. Yes No. 2

14.9 Explain your answer
....

Questionnaire For University Staff

We are from the Centre for Development Studies, University of Cape Coast. We are conducting a study on sexual harassment in Ghanaian public universities. The study seeks to investigate the incidence, nature and forms of sexual harassment as exists on the university campuses in Ghana. You have been randomly selected to be part of the study. Your response to the questions about to be posed to you will provide vital information for the eventual development of an effective framework for managing sexual harassment in this university. The information you give us will be kept confidential; no one will ever know what you said. We will like to crave your indulgence and cooperation for your time as you answer these questions.

Time interview started [   ]

SECTION 1 Respondent's Background

We will like to begin by asking you questions about yourself.

1.1 Sex 1. Female [...] 2. Male [...]

1.2 Religion 1. Christianity[...] 2. Islamic[...] 3. Traditional [...]
4. No religion[...] 5. Others (specify)

1.3 Nationality

1.4   Educational Background (highest level attained)

    1. None   6. Training College

    2. Non formal   7. Polytechnic

    3. Elementary/JSS   8. University

    4. Vocational   9. Other Tertiary (Specify)

    5. Secondary/Technical

1.5   In what year and month were you born year [........]   month [........]

1.6   Marital Status   1. Married [...] 2. Single [...] 3. Divorced [...]
    4. Widowed/widower [...]   5. Separated [...] 6. Consensual [...]

1.7   Are you a member of any type of group or association or organisation which meets regularly (Tick appropriate column)

Associations	On-Campus	Off-Campus
Social grouping		
Political grouping		
Ethnic grouping		
Academic grouping		
Professional grouping		
Other (specify)		

1.8   What section or department do you belong to in this university?

1.9   What is your Position .... rank? ....

1.10   In what year and month did you begin work in this university? Month......... Year..........

1.11   In what year and month did you begin work in this section/dept? Month...... Year.......

1.12   What type of work do you do here? ....

SECTION 2 Defining sexual harassment and setting limits

2.1   What to you constitutes sexual harassment?

2.2   Which behaviours will you classify as sexual harassment?

2.3   How do people here generally define sexual harassment?

2.3   What behaviours do people here generally describe as sexual harassment

SECTION 3 Attitudes About Sexual Harassment

People in the university community find themselves in situations where they

get easily sexually harassed. Some people believe that sexual harassment can be avoided and some people get sexually harassed because they invited it on themselves. Some people also believe that sexual harassment is an alien concept and most of the things people label as sexual harassment are culturally acceptable in Ghana. Which of the following acts do you think are unacceptable and should carry the name sexual harassment

3.14   Verbal abuse about sexual habits by a colleague or peer [...]
3.15   Sexist remarks about a woman's body [...]
3.16   Sexist remarks about a woman's clothing [...]
3.17   Sexist remarks about a woman's sexual habits [...]
3.18   Subtle pressure for sex [...]
3.19   Suggestive gestures alluding to sex [...]
3.20   Lurid jokes about sex to females [...]
3.21   Uninvited touching, [...]
3.22   Uninvited patting, pinching [...]
3.23   Uninvited fondling [...]
3.24   Uninvited rubbing grabbing, [...]
3.25   Uninvited kissing, [...]
3.26   Demand for sexual favours under a veiled threat for a job or academic favours [...]

SECTION 4 Causes/Sources

4.1   *Here is a list of factors that have been noted to promote sexual harassment in other universities. Which of these factors are likely to attract sexual harassment on campus here? You can give 1 to the factor you consider most likely to attract sexual harassment and 2 to the next and so on.*

— Admissions into programmes in the university   [...]
— A basis for offering some form of academic support   [...]
— Passing end of semester examinations   [...]
— Getting a good grade in examinations   [...]
— Appointment into the employment of the university   [...]
— Promotion into a higher rank   [...]
— Renewal of contract   [...]
— Post retirement contract   [...]
— When some females want to contest high office on campus [...]

4.2   What factors do you think encourage some people to harass others?
4.3   How will you explain the occurrence of sexual harassment in this university?
4.4   Admissions into some programmes of the university are generally

believed to attract more instances of sexual harassment than others.

    1. Yes   2. No

4.5   Please explain your answer

4.6   Sexual harassment is used to deter females from holding high office in this university.   1. Yes   2. No

4.7   The balance between the sexes in a particular department can encourage sexual harassment   1. Yes 2. No

4.7   Which of the following balance is the cause of sexual harassment in the section/dept that you belong to?

    1. Females are too few   3. Too many males

    2. Males are too few   4. Too many females

SECTION 5 Assumptions about Sexual Harassment

5.1   Who do you think is more likely to be sexually harassed?

    1. Females   2. Males   3. Explain your answer

5.2   Do females and males have the same experience of sexual harassment?

    1. Yes   2. No

5.3   Do males also experience sexual harassment? 1. Yes   2. No

5.4   What behaviours do men generally consider as sexually harassing?

5.5   What behaviours do you think females generally consider as sexual harassment?

5.6   Do you believe that some behaviour of women generally have the tendency to invite sexual harassment? 1. Yes   2. No

5.7   Explain your answer.

5.8   Can females adopt behaviours that can ward off sexual harassment?

5.9   Do males sexually harass other males? 1. Yes   2. No

5.10   In what ways can males sexually harass other males?

5.11   Do females sexually harass other males? 1. Yes   2. No

5.12   In what ways can females sexually harass males?

5.13   Members of the university community most likely to suffer sexual harassment (Please fill in the appropriate codes below)

	Code	Explain
Categories of males most likely to face harassment from females		
Categories of males most likely to face harassment from males		
Categories of females most likely to face harassment from females		
Categories of females most likely to face harassment from males		

Codes 1. Students 2. Lecturers 3. Teaching Assistants 4. Senior Staff
     5. Junior Staff 6. Others specify (e.g. Landlords, etc.).....................

5.14   Which department/section of the university community is sexual harassment most likely to occur? ......

5.15   Can people adopt behaviours that will enable them ward off sexual harassment?   1. Yes   2. No

5.16   Explain your answer.

SECTION 6. Female/Male Experience of Sexual Harassment
Please specify you what you think about the following statements by indicating whether you strongly agree (SA=4), agree (A=3), disagree (D=2), strongly disagree (SDA =1) in the boxes provided

Female/Male Experience of Sexual Harassment	1	2	3	4
6.1 More women than men face harassment				
6.2 Women will not be sexually harassed if they learnt to behave themselves				
6.3 Women generally face harassment because of the way they dress				
6.4 It is only a certain type of woman who gets harassed				
6.5 Women generally can prevent sexual harassment if they resisted male sexually advances hard enough				
6.6 Most of the time when women say no they mean yes men only have to press hard				
6.7 Some females are not offended by sexually harassing events they even enjoy them				
6.8 Females who learn to keep away from certain places do not suffer sexual harassment				
6.9 Some females only exaggerate and even tell lies about being sexually harassed				
6.10 It is only a certain type of person who sexually harass others				
6.11 Males who harass others are sick or ill or even under some form of stress				
6.12 Complimenting a woman does not constitute sexual harassment				
6.13 Most women who experience sexual harassment ask for it				
6.14 Female students who engage in commercial sex are more likely to be sexually harassed Female/Male Experience of Sexual Harassment				

Female/Male Experience of Sexual Harassment	1	2	3	4
6.15 Once a student is involved in commercial sex she should not complain if she finds herself being sexually harassed				
6.16 The body language and attitudes of women tends to invite sexual harassment from males				
6.17 Some people take advantage of certain circumstances to sexually harass others				
6.18 Some people behave in a certain way in order to avoid being sexually harassed				
6.19 The way people perceive women is carried from home to the workplace				
6.20 The perceptions people have about the roles women/men perform at home does influence the way jobs are assigned in this department/section/institute				
6.21 Whatever the level of education a woman has attained her status as a woman should reflect in her relationship or dealings with males in her workplace				
6.22 Perceptions about women and their social roles always feature prominently in how they are related to in the workplace				
6.23. Women tend to be better at performing certain task than men				
6.24 Women at the work place should be assigned certain task and not others				
6.25 Women are only fit for certain positions in this university and not others				
6.26 Women are not assertive and they can be easily manipulated by men they should therefore not be allowed to head any department or section in this university				

Female/Male Experience of Sexual Harassment	1	2	3	4
6.27 Qualification is a secondary issue in the advancement of women in this university. Other factors such as a relationship with a male superior officer can help pave the way for career advancement in this university				
6.28 Societal roles and perceptions about women are important factors in assigning jobs and recruiting women in this department or section				

Section 7. Personal Experience of Sexual Harassment

The next batch of questions cover an area that might bring some discomfort for you. Ever so often in our lives we do have experiences that tend to be painful or embarrassing. The questions cover ways in which people harass other people and possible ways you might have been harassed yourself. Please do try to be as open as and truthful as possible. As you are already aware the answers you provide will be treated as secrets and no one will ever know that you have said anything.

7.1 Have you ever had any experience that you consider sexually harassing? 1. Yes 2. No

7.2. How often do you face this kind of experience? (Please state number of times within a semester ?)

7.3 Who are the perpetrators? Please indicate sex......... rank...... .... and position or status of the perpetrators (name not required)

7.4 Please describe any such experience/s you have had which you consider sexually harassing.

7.5 Where did this experience occur? ....

7.6 When was the last time you had such an experience? ....

7.7 What do you think was the cause of the experience? ....

7.8 What was your reaction?...

7.9 What effect did the experience have on you? ....

7.10 Did you report? 1. Yes 2. No

7.11 If yes, who did you report to? ....

7.12 If yes, What action was taken? ....

7.13   Were you satisfied with the type of action taken?   1. Yes   2. No

7.14   Explain your answer. ....

7.15   If you did not report, why ? ....

7.16   Do you find your self being continuously harassed ?(Multiple response)

    1.   By the same group of people? (specify................................)

    2.   By a particular person? (Specify e.g. boyfriend etc.....................)

7.17   What behaviours of yours generally have been interpreted as an invitation to harass you?

7.18   Do you generally experience any of the following? If you do indicate the source of the experience and how often it happens to you in a week/month/year as well as where it occurs

Experience	Source	Location	Frequency
	(Type of person)	*(Place)*	*(No. of times)*
➤ Unwanted touching	....	....	....
➤ Cat calls	....	....	....
➤ Rubbing	....	....	....
➤ Booing and jeers	....	....	....
➤ Kissing & grabbing	....	....	....
➤ Name calling	....	....	....
➤ Fondling	....	....	....
➤ Teasing	....	....	....
➤ Exposure to pornography	....	....	....
➤ Sexual jokes	....	....	....

7.19   Has any one hinted that you could lose your job or that your work might be hurt if you did not meet some demands like a date or sex?

    1. Yes   2. No

7.20   Please explain. ....

7.21   As a child did anyone at school ever give you any attention you considered sexual that made you uncomfortable?   1. Yes

    2. No

7.22   If yes how often was this experience?...

7.23   Who (rank/position and relationship to you) gave you this attention?

    ....

7.24   What was your reaction? ....

7.25   Why did you react in this way?...

7.26   As you were growing up did any teacher/lecturer ever hint that you could improve your exams or get bad marks or that your schooling would be damaged if you did not meet some sexual demand like sex or a date?
      1. Yes   2. No

7.27   Please explain ....

7.28   Has any one ever forced or persuaded you to have sex against your will by threatening, holding you down or hurting you in some way?
      1. Yes   .   2. No

7.29   When did this happen to you? ....

7.30   Who did this to you (name not required state status and position as well as relationship to respondent)?

7.31   Has any man ever insisted that you should have sex with him before he would give you a job in this university? 1. Yes   2. No

7.32   Do you know of any one who has experienced sexual harassment? 1. Yes
        2. No

7.33   Sex .... position...............and department ....of person

7.34   What was the nature of this experience? ....

7.35   Who did the person report the experience to and why? ....

7.36   What was the nature of action that was given? ....

7.37   Was the person who suffered the harassment satisfied with the action?
      1. Yes   2. No

7.38   What did the person do? ....

7.39   What would you have done if it were you? ....

7.40   Have you ever reported any experience of sexual harassment that you had to any one?
      1. Yes   2. No

7.41   Who did you report to? ....

7.42   Why?...

7.43   How long have you been experiencing sexual harassment before you decided to report?

7.44   What made you decide to report to the body/person you reported to?
      ....

7.45   What action was taken? ....

7.46   What action were you advised to take? ....

7.47   What action did you take? ....

7.48   What sanctions did the person harassing you get?
      ....

7.49   Were you happy about the disciplinary action taken? 1. Yes   2. No

7.50   If you had to decide what punishment the person should get what would you decide?

7.51   Did you withdraw the charges after reporting? 1. Yes   2. No

7.52   Why did you withdraw the charges? ....

7.53   Did any one threaten or put pressure on you to withdraw the charges?
       1. Yes   2. No

7.54   If yes, explain what happened. ....

7.55   Did you seek for help?   1. Yes   2. No

7.56   Explain your answer. ....

7.57   Did any one intervene on your behalf to end the harassing experience?
       1. Yes   2. No

7.58   Who did? Position and rank of person (Name not required)
       ....

7.59   If you found that you had a sexually harassing problem who would you feel comfortable talking to?

SECTION 8. Impact

8.1   If you have experienced sexual harassment describe the effect it had on you.

8.2   Were others around you affected by the experience? 1. Yes   2. No

8.3   If yes in what ways were they affected by your experience/how were they affected?

8.4   If you know of someone who has experienced sexual harassment describe the effect it had on this person. How does the knowledge that some colleague is facing sexual harassment affect you and other colleagues? Are some people compelled to tolerate sexual harassment because of the fear that they might lose some academic or professional favour?
       1. Yes   2. No

8.5   How far is it true that if one does not give in to sexual advances in this university one's career advancement might be compromised.
       ....

8.6   Are people here generally able to defy the odds and reject sexual harassment despite the problems their action might pose for their own career? 1. Yes   2. No

8.7   Explain. ....

8.8   Does the fear of going through a sexually harassing experience ever intimidate you? 1. Yes   2. No

8.9   Please explain your answer. ....

8.10   Do you find yourself doing certain things in order to avoid getting sexually harassed? 1. Yes   2. No

8.11   Please explain your answer. ....

SECTION 9. Occupational Situation and Sexual Harassment
9.1   What barriers exist in this dept/section that prevent people from advancing
       in their jobs as a result of their sex?
9.2   Do women and men with equal qualification enjoy the same benefits in
       terms of the following provisions? (Tick the appropriate column)

Benefits	Equal	In favour of females	In favour of males	Reasons
Accommodation				
Salary advance				
Vehicle loans				
Absence for study leave				
Training				
Out of station duty assignments				
Medical claims for children and spouse				

9.3   Do both men and women have the same chances of getting promoted in
       this department/section?   1. Yes   2. No
9.4   What prevents women as a group from getting promoted in this section/
       department? ....
9.5   Have you ever faced any barriers in terms of career advancement in your
       work here?   1. Yes   2. No
9.6   Do you personally think that a woman should endure a job situation
       where she is sexually harassed for the sake of keeping her job or
       advancing in her career? 1. Yes   2. No
9.7   Explain your answer. ....
9.8   Do you think that it is right for any one to intervene on behalf of this
       woman?   1. Yes 2. No
9.9   If yes, state who should intervene. ....
9.10   Do you think that your job assignments measure up to your specialisation
       and qualification? 1. Yes   2. No
9.11   Explain your answer please. ....

SECTION 10. Sexual habits; Sexuality and Commercial Sex

10.1   Is it proper for female to have sex with someone she is not married to? 1. Yes 2. No

10.2   Explain your answer. ....

10.3   Do you think that it is proper for a male to have sex with someone he is not married to?   1. Yes   2. No

10.4   Explain your answer. ....

10.5   Do you think that when females say no to sexual advances they really mean no? 1. Yes   2. No

10.6   Explain your answer ....

10.7   Does the fact that a relationship is going steady entitle a boy to have sex with his girl friend any time he feels like it? 1. Yes   2. No

10.8   Which of these do you consider to be more serious?
       1.   Married woman suffering sexual harassment
       2.   Unmarried woman suffering sexual harassment

SECTION 11. Making Sexual Harassment Visible

11.1   In your opinion do think that the number of cases of sexual harassment that we get to hear about is a true reflection of the amount of sexual harassment cases that are experienced on this campus? 1. Yes   2. No .

11.2   Why do you say that? ....

11.3   Where do you think that all who experience sexual harassment report their experience?

11.4   Do you think that all who experience sexual harassment report their experience?

11.5   If not why do you think that people are not reporting their experience of sexual harassment?

11.6   If you do experience sexual harassment would you prefer that the person you talk to comes from the
       1. Same ethnic group   2. Religious group   3. Social group
       4. Political group

11.7   Why? ....

11.8   If you did experience sexual harassment would you prefer that the person you talked to comes from the
       1. Same ethnic group   2. Religious group   3. Social group
       4. Political group

11.9   Explain your answer. ....

SECTION 12. The University Regulatory System

12.1   Do you know of any rules/regulations within the university for dealing specifically with sexual harassment? 1. Yes   2. No

12.2   If yes what is it? ....

12.3   Where can this rules and regulations be found? ....

12.4   What sections/departments are responsible for handling sexual harassment?

12.5   Have you ever had to use the services of the section or departments responsible for handling sexual harassment? 1. Yes   2. No

12.6   If yes state the particular unit that you used. ....

12.7   Were you satisfied with the assistance you received? 1. Yes   2. No

12.8   Would you use this system again if you had a similar experience?
       1. Yes   2. No

12.9   Explain your answer? ....

12.10 Would you recommend this system to any one who has a sexual harassment problem? 1. Yes   2. No

12.11 Explain your answer? ....

SECTION 13. Group Dynamism and Sexual Harassment
Please specify you what you think about the following statements by indicating whether you strongly agree (SA=4), agree (A=3), disagree (D=2), strongly disagree (SDA=1) in the boxes provided

Female/Male Experience of Sexual Harassment	1	2	3	4
13.1 It is not right to report a sexual harassment offence perpetrated by someone from your own tribe knowing that the person might lose his/her education?				
13.2 Some girls have a habit of accusing some people from some religious groups or ethnic groups as likely harassers.				
13.3 Some girls likely to be victims of harassment because they belong to a particular ethnic or religious group				
13.4 If members of a disciplinary team belong to the same ethnic/religious group as you then you will be more likely to receive a fair hearing at in a sexual harassment suit				
13.5 People generally will not report their experience of sexual harassment because a member of their tribe/ethnic group might lose his/her education				

	1	2	3	4
13.6 Some people have a habit of accusing some people of sexually harassing them because those people belong to a particular ethnic/ religious group				
13.7 Some members of some ethnic group are more likely to harass women because of the way females are valued in their ethnic group				
13.8 The way women are presented in some cultures makes them easy prey for sexual harassers				
13.9 Some people are likely to be victims of harassment because they belong to a particular ethnic/religious group				
13.10 If members of a disciplinary team belonged to the same ethnic/religious group as you will you be more likely to receive a fair hearing in a sexual harassment case				

SECTION 14. Conclusion

14.1   What do you think should be done to end sexual harassment in this university?

14.2   Is there anything else that you will want to say about the sexual harassment that this interview did not cover?................................

14.3   Before we finish can you say a few words about what you thought about the subject that we have just discussed? ....

14.4   Were all the issues that you thought are important to sexual harassment in this university covered in this interview?   1. Yes   2. No

14.5   What additional comments do you have to make about this interview?

14.6   Do you think that there are a lot of these kinds of problems in this area? 1. Yes   2. No

14.7   Explain your answer. ....

14.8   Do you think people would come out and talk about their sexually harassing experience to researchers in this study? 1. Yes   2. No

14.9   Explain your answer...

SECTION 15. Interviewer's Report

15.1 Is the interview complete? 1. Yes 2. No

15.2 How would you rate the overall quality of this interview?
1. Very poor 4. Somewhat good
2. Somewhat poor 5. Very good
3. Neither poor nor good

15.3 Overall, would you say that the respondent's reaction to the interview was positive?
1. Very negative 4. Somewhat positive
2. Somewhat negative 5. Very positive
3. Neither negative nor positive

15.4 Overall, how sincere did the respondent seem to be in his/her answers?
1. Very insincere 3. Neither insincere nor sincere
2. Somewhat insincere 4. Somewhat sincere 5. Very sincere

Key Persons Interview Guide

We are from the Centre for Development Studies, University of Cape Coast. We are conducting a study on sexual harassment in Ghanaian public universities. The study seeks to investigate the incidence, nature and forms of sexual harassment as exists on the university campuses in Ghana. You have been randomly selected to be part of the study. Your response to the questions about to be posed to you will provide vital information for the eventual development of an effective framework for managing sexual harassment in our universities. The information you give us will be kept confidential. We will like to crave your indulgence and cooperation for your time as you answer these questions.

Interviewer's codes

Instrument code

Time interview began

Section 1 Respondent's Background
We will begin by asking questions about yourself
1.1 Sex 1. Female 2. Male
1.2 Religion 1. Christianity [...] 2. Islamic [...] 3. Traditional [...]
4. No religion [...] 5. Others (specify) ....
1.3 Nationality...
1.4 Position.......................................Rank............................
1.5 In what year and month were you born? year[........] month [........]
1.6 Marital status 1. Married/living together 2. Divorced 3. Separated
4. Single 5. Widower/Widowed 6. Consensual
1.7 Are you a member of any type of group or association or organization

which meets regularly? (Tick appropriate column)

Associations	On-Campus	Off-Campus
Social grouping		
Political grouping		
Ethnic grouping		
Academic grouping		
Professional grouping		
Other (specify)		

1.8   What is your understanding of sexual harassment? ....

1.9   What forms of behaviours would you generally classify as sexual harassment?

1.10   How often do you receive complaints about sexual harassment in this department/section within a week?

·1.11   What forms of sexual harassment do you receive reports on?

1.12   Who are the people who experience these forms of harassment?

1.13   Who are the perpetrators?

1.14   What department/sections are responsible for handling sexual harassment complaints?

1.15   Have you ever had to use the services of this department/ section?
1. Yes   2. No

1.16   If yes, then state the particular department/section/unit. ....

1.17   Is your department/section/unit responsible for handling sexual harassment complaints?   1. Yes   2. No

1.18   What structures do you have in place for these complaints?

1.19   What actions have your section/department taken in relation to such complaints?

1.20   Are you satisfied with the structures you have in place?   1. Yes
2. No

1.21   Please explain your answer. ....

1.22   Which department/sections of the university community are most vulnerable to sexual harassment?

1.23   Do you know of any provision within the university for dealing specifically with sexual harassment?   1. Yes   2. No.

1.24   What do you think can be done to strengthen the existing structures for dealing with sexual harassment in this university? ....

1.25   If you have to set up any structures to manage sexual harassment in this university, what kind of structures would you put in place? ....

1.26   What do you think should be done to end sexual harassment in this university?

1.27   Is there anything else that you will want to say about the sexual harassment that this interview/questionnaire did not cover? ....

1.28   Before we finish can you say a few words about what you thought about the subject that we have just discussed? ....

1.29   Were all the issues that you thought are important to sexual harassment in this university covered in this interview?   1. Yes   2. No

1.30   What additional comments do you have to make about this interview?

1.31   Do you think that there are a lot of these kinds of problems in this area?
        1. Yes   2. No

1.32   Explain your answer. ....

1.33   Do you think people would come out and talk about their sexually harassing experiences to researchers in this study? 1. Yes   2. No

1.34   Explain your answer. ....

INTERVIEWER'S REPORT

1.35   Is the interview complete?   1. Yes   2. No

1.36   How would you rate the overall quality of this interview?
        1. Very poor   4. Somewhat good
        2. Somewhat poor   5. Very good
        3. Neither poor nor good

1.37   Overall, would you say that the respondent's reaction to the interview was positive?
        1. Very negative   4. Somewhat positive
        2. Somewhat negative   5. Very positive
        3. Neither negative nor positive

1.38   Overall, how sincere did the respondent seem to be in his/her answers?
        1. Very insincere   4. Somewhat sincere
        2. Somewhat insincere   5. Very sincere
        3. Neither insincere nor sincere

Group Interview Schedule

1. What is your understanding of sexual harassment
2. What behaviours will you identify as sexual harassment
3. How will you describe the level of incidence of sexual harassment in this university?
4. What factors do you think are the causes of sexual harassment in this university?
5. Which members of the university community are most likely to suffer sexual harassment?
6. What do you think about the way sexual harassment cases are handled on campus presently?
7. What rules and regulations cover sexual harassment in this university?
8. What suggestions do you have for improving upon the way sexual harassment cases are handled currently?
9. People believe that accusations of sexual harassment are difficult to establish. What is your position about this?
10. If you were given the opportunity to determine how sexual harassment cases should be handled on this campus what suggestion would you offer?
11. Do you think that a certain kind of behaviour attracts sexual harassment?
12. Do you think that a person can ward off sexual harassment by behaving in a certain way?
13. How have people who experience sexual harassment tried to resist the harassment?
14. How do people generally try to cope with sexual harassment in this university?
15. What specific financial needs do students have on this campus?
16. How do people try to meet these needs?
17. Do students consider commercial sex as an option? What categories of students are likely to be involved in commercial sex?
18. What is the general attitude of the university community to members who are suspected to be involved in commercial sex?
19. How far are people who are suspected of being involved in commercial sex likely to get sexually harassed?
20. How can sexual harassment be stopped in this university?

APPENDIX 5

WORKSHOP GROUP DISCUSSION GUIDES

GROUP ONE

Regulations to Uphold the Basic Rights of Members of the University Community

- ♀ How should we define sexual harassment and what behaviours should be sanctioned?
- ♀ What will be appropriate sanctions for sexual harassment offences?
- ♀ What resources will be required to enforce these sanctions?
- ♀ Which concerns can best provide justification for a sexual harassment policy in the university:
  - Equal opportunity
  - Academic excellence
  - Human rights
  - Gender rights
- ♀ Which section/unit/department should have responsibility for sexual harassment regulation?
- ♀ What should be the relationship of sanction to other state legal systems e.g. courts, WAJU, CHRAJ,
- ♀ What minimum inputs will show proof of the university's commitment to upholding the basic rights of it's members to an environment free of sexual harassment?

GROUP TWO

Grievance procedure for effective, prompt and equitable resolution of sexual harassment complaints
- What should be the complaints procedure?
- What should be the investigative procedure?
- What monitoring mechanisms should be put in place to ensure enforcement?
- What resources will be required for:
  - Complainants
  - Investigative team (human and material)
  - Complaints office (human and material)
  - Monitoring team (human and material)
- What minimum inputs will show proof of the university's commitment to providing an effective, prompt and equitable resolution of all sexual harassment complaints?

GROUP THREE

University based strategies for empowering vulnerable members and changing beliefs and attitudes that promote sexual harassment
- What strategies should be evolved to empower vulnerable members of the university community in terms of:
  - Reaching out to different sections of the university community
  - Reaching out to other non-members of the university community who operate on the university campus (taxi-drivers, operators of commercial units, landlords & ladies where non-resident students live)
  - Offering support to complainants when they are going through the investigation procedure

- What strategies should be set in place to deal with the environment in work and teaching situations that encourage the occurrence of sexual harassment like:
  - Sexual bribery and
  - Sexual corruption
  - Students' traditions and celebrations

ၣ What strategies should be evolved to change the beliefs and attitudes of
- Possible harassers
- The vulnerable
- Personnel responsible for effecting the policy

ၣ What structures and facilities should be set up to support the strategies suggested

ၣ What minimum inputs will show proof of the university's commitment to evolving strategies for:
- Empowering vulnerable and
- Changing beliefs and attitudes towards sexual harassment?

REFERENCES

Aeberhard-Hodges J. 1997 "Unwelcome, unwanted and increasing Illegal Sexual Harassment in the Workplace" in ILO *World of Work* The Magazine of the ILO, No. 19 Geneva: ILO.

African Women Lawyers Association (AWLA Ghana) 2003. *Report of a Survey on the incidence of Sexual Harassment in Ghana.* Unpublished Research Report.

African Women Lawyers Association (AWLA Ghana) 2003. *Dealing With Sexual Harassment in the Workplace and School: A Checklist of Best Practices.* Unpublished Research Report.

Bhasin Kamla 1993. *What is Patriarchy?* New Delhi; Kali for Women.

Bortei-Doku- Aryeetey, Ellen 2004. *Coming to Terms with Sexual Harassment in Ghana.* Technical Publication No. 64, ISSER, University of Ghana, Legon.

Bortei-Doku- Aryeetey, Ellen and Kuenyehia Akua. 1999. Violence against Women in Ghana. In Akua Kuenyehia. Ed. *Women and Law in West Africa: Situational Analysis of Some Key Issues Affecting Women.* Accra: Yamens

Brandt, Claire and Too Yun Lee (eds) 1994. *Rethinking Sexual Harassment.* London: Pluto Press

Brown C. K., Nana A. Anokye and Akua O. Britwum. 1996. *Women in Public Life.* Accra: Friedrich Ebert Foundation.

Coker-Appiah, Dorcas and Kathy Cusack (eds.) 1999. *Violence Against Women & Children in Ghana: Report of a National Study on Violence.* Accra: Gender Centre & Human Rights Documentation Centre.

Commission of European Communities 1993. *How to Combat Sexual Harassment at work: A Guide to Implementing the European Commission Code of Practice.* Luxemburg: Union of Shop, Distributive and Allied Workers.

Dall'Ara, Elena and Maass Anne 1999. Studying Sexual Harassment in the Laboratory; Are Egalitarian Women at Higher Risk? *Email Journal of Research*

Daily Graphic, October 15, 2001 "Legon Students Kick Against Indecent Dress"

Dawene, Edoja Solomon 1985. *Perception of Sexual harassment in Institutions of Higher Learning: A Case Study of the College of Education of Ilorin.* A Research Project Submitted in Partial fulfilment for the Award of the Degree of Bachelor of Education in the Department of Guidance and Counselling of the Faculty of Education, University of Ilorin, Nigeria.

Desouza Eros R. and John B Pryor, Claudio S Hutz 1998. Reactions to Sexual Harassment   Charges Between North Americans and Brazilians *Email Journal of Research.*

Dobash Emerson R. and Russel P. Dobash 1992. *Women Violence and Social Change.* London: Rutledge

Fiscian, Vivian Sarpomaa, Fiona Leach and Leslie Casely-Hayford. 2003. *An Investigative Study of Abuse of Girls in Ghanaian Basic Schools.* DFID

Fitzgerald L. and Shullman, S. L. 1993. "Sexual Harassment: A Research Analysis and Agenda for the 1990s," *Journal of Vocational Behaviour.* 42, 5-27

Good Kenneth 1999.   Sexual harassment and the academy: Two contrasting case studies. *University of Botswana Centre for Academic Development Bulletin,* No. 16, 16-19

Guiffre, Patti A. and Williams, Christine L. 1994. Boundary Lines: Labelling Sexual Harassment In Restaurants Gender and *Society Vol. No. 3*

Heise Lori, Ellsberg M. and Gottenmoeller, M. 1999. Ending Violence Against Women, *Population Reports Series.* No 11, population Information Programme of the School of Public Health, Johns Hopkins University. Population Information Programme

Heise Lori, Kirsten Moore, Mahid Touba 1995. *Sexual Coercion and Reproductive Health: A Focus on Reproductive Research.* New York: The Population Council.

Henry Jeanne and Julian Meltzoff 1998. *Perceptions of Sexual Harassment as a function of Target's Response Type and Observer's Sex. Kluwer Academic Publishers Issue 3/4 (253-271)*

Hughes, J and Sandler B 1988. "Peer Harassment: Hassles for Women of Campus," Report from the Project on the Status of Women. Washington DC.

ILO 1994. *Women Workers Rights: Modular Training Package. Equality for Women in Employment:*   an Inter-department Project. Geneva, ILO.

Jansen I. W. and Gutek B. A. 1982. "Attributes and Assignment of Responsibility," *Journal of Social Issues.* 38, 4 12-136

Kelly, Liz. 1988. *Surviving Sexual Violence.* Cambridge, Polity Press

Koss Mary P. and Cleveland, Hobart 1997. "Stepping on Toes: Social Roots of Date Rape Lead to Intractability and Politicization". In Martin D. Schwartz *Researching Sexual Violence Against 140 Women: Methodological and Personal Perspectives.* London: SAGE Publications

Livingstone J.A. 1982. "Responses to Sexual Harassment on the Job: Legal, Organisational and Individual Actions" *Journal of Social Issues.* 38,4; (5-22)

McKinnon C. A .1979. *Sexual Harassment of Working Women: A Case of Sex Discrimination.* New Haven Connecticut: Yale University Press.

Micah J. A., Akua O. Britwum and Nana Amma Anokye 1998. "Sexual Harassment in Tertiary Institutions: the Case to the University of Cape Coast." Proceedings of a Workshop organised by the Centre for Development Studies, University of Cape Coast; December 1998.

Pereira, Charmaine 2002. "Between Knowing and Imagining: What Space for Feminism in Scholarship on Africa," GWS Feminist Africa Launch Issue.

Public Agenda. 1999. Special Pullout on Sexual Harassment. May 24-30th.

Reilly T, Carpenter VD, and Bertdet K 1982. "The Factoral Survey: An Approach to Defining Sexual Harassment on Campus," *In Journal of Social Issues* 3, 4. (99-111).

Reinhart Ariane 1999. *Sexual Harassment: Addressing Sexual harassment In the Workplace—A Management Information Booklet.* Geneva: International Labour Organization.

Reddi, Managay. 2003. "Sexual harassment in the Workplace: Do we Need New Legislation?" In Bowman, Cynthia Grant and Kuenyehia Akua. (eds) *Women and Law in Sub-Saharan Africa.* Accra: Sedco.(564-571)

Stein, Nan 1993. *Secrets in Public: Sexual Harassment In Public (Private) Schools,* Working Paper Series No 256; Wellesley College.

Twumasi, Nana Efua. 2002. *Sexual Harassment and Clothing: A Case Study of the University of Cape Coast,* University of Cape Coast: Unpublished Student Dissertation

University of Botswana, *Sexual Harassment Policy Procedures;* University of Botswana 2001/2002 Calendar 37-40.

University of Cape Town. 1991. *Final Report of the Committee of Enquiry into Sexual Harassment.* Equal Opportunity Research Project. University of Cape Town, Cape Town.

University of Cape Town 1994   *Challenging Sexual Harassment: A Conference on Strategies within Tertiary Education.* Sexual Harassment Prevention and Support Service and the Equal Opportunity Research Project of the University of Cape Town.

University of Cape Coast: University Basic Statistics 2000

University of Cape Coast. *Corporate Strategy* January 2003

University College of Education: Winneba, *University BasicStatistics; 2000*

University of Ghana: *University Basic Statistics: 2000*

University for Development Studies: *University Basic Statistics: 2000*

Wamahiu Sheila P and Fatuma Chege: 1996 "Empowering Strategy For Dealing with Sexual Harassment and Abuse: A Case Study From Kenya." Paper Prepared for the African Conference on the Empowerment of Women through Functional Literacy and Education of the Girl Child, Sept 8-13 1996, Kampala, Uganda.

Women in USDAW *Tackling Sexual Harassment:* USDAW Education Training for Action:

Young Kate 1993. *Planning Development with Women: Making A World of Difference.* London: Macmillan

List of Dissemination Workshop Reports

Report on Dissemination Workshop on "Confronting Sexual Harassment in Ghanaian Public" University of Cape Coast 7th April 2003

Report on Dissemination Workshop on "Confronting Sexual Harassment in Ghanaian Public" University of Ghana; 10th April 2003.

Report on Dissemination Workshop on "Confronting Sexual Harassment in Ghanaian Public" Kwame Nkrumah University of Science and Technology; 22nd April 2003.

Report on Dissemination Workshop on "Confronting Sexual Harassment in Ghanaian Public" University for Development Studies; 24th April 2003.

Report on Dissemination Workshop on "Confronting Sexual Harassment in Ghanaian Public" University of Education Winneba; 26th May 2003.